AMAZING Bible RACE ™

Law

Genesis— Deuteronomy

Leg 1

09   10   11   12   13   14   15   16—10   9   8   7   6   5

Cover Design: Keely Moore

Contents

© 2007 by Abingdon Press

Welcome to The Amazing Bible Race! With your team, you are about to embark on the race of a lifetime. You'll get to read the entire Bible. How many adults can say that they have done that? You will enter the Bible stories and discover new truths about God and about yourself on this race. You'll explore ancient lands, people, and promises that have a direct connection to who you are and how you practice your faith today. This is amazing stuff!

As you prepare yourself for the Race, keep a few things in mind:

1. **Be a team player**—Lean on your team to get you through difficult passages and hurdles. Work together to make this a great experience. Don't let any of your teammates wander off; make sure everyone stays on track.

2. **Give it your all**—Sure, you could do this Race halfway. You could read a little bit, take some quizzes on the website, walk a little bit outside your team; but you wouldn't get all you could out of it. Think of this as a marathon to the heart of God. Seek God in the Bible, and learn who and whose you are!

3. **Focus on the journey, not on the prize**—True, there are points earned for each daily reading, weekly challenge, hurdle, fast forward, and extra web quiz. The points keep you on target and help you gauge your progress. And true, there may be prizes along the way. But this race isn't about the points or the prize. It's about meeting God in the Bible. It's about sealing the Scriptures on your heart. Give yourself to that mission, and you are a winner!

4. **Use a Bible translation that you understand**—If you take in the Scriptures better by listening to them online, do that. If you prefer reading more scholarly translations, read the *NRSV* or *NIV*. If you prefer to read more contemporary language, choose the *CEV* or *TNIV*. There may even be times when you'll need to read *The Message* paraphrase of the Bible to fully understand the passage. Read what you understand so that you can understand what you read.

AMAZING Bible RACE

The Rules

Rule 1
Follow steps 1–4 for each daily reading.

Rule 2
As a team, answer the Weekly Challenges and submit it to the website.

Rule 3
Accomplish any Fast Forwards that appear in your Runner's Reader. A Fast Forward appears periodically and is a life-application exercise for your team. You'll be asked to find a way to apply the Bible reading to your life today. For example, if you're reading about feeding the hungry, you might decide to serve food at a homeless shelter. To receive credit for the outing, you must have someone make a video of it or take a photo of your group in action, then upload it on *amazingbiblerace.com*.

Rule 4
Help your teammates overcome any Hurdles. When you face a particularly difficult section of Scripture or feel that you're getting stuck, you might see a Hurdle. Hurdles allow you to skim that particular Scripture passage and accomplish or perform a task based on the Bible lesson or solve a quiz on *amazingbiblerace.com* to "quiz-out" of that section.

Rule 5
Earn as many points as possible for your team. You gain points by finishing your daily readings, solving Weekly Challenges, participating in the Fast Forwards, solving the extra quizzes, or looking on the map and taking a quiz. The more effort you put into the Race, the more you'll get out of it—and the more points you'll receive!

Rule 6
The adult mentor is the team coach who keeps team members encouraged and motivated. The coach should check in at least once a week to make sure that everyone is reading and that you have a time scheduled to work together (by IM, e-mail, text message, or phone conversation) to solve the Weekly Challenge.

Rule 7
Support your team and work together.

Rule 8
Have fun!

In the Beginning
Genesis 1–2

1 Scouting the Terrain

Most of us know that the first two chapters of the Bible tell the story of how God created the heavens and earth. God created everything— blah, blah, blah—and that's the basic point, right? *Wrong.* Because we're so familiar with the story of Adam and Eve and how God made the world in seven days, it's easy to skim over the details of these first two chapters. Therefore, we miss a whole lot of important information about who God is; what type of attitude we should have about work; how God initially encouraged us to eat; and what some of the very first gifts were from God to us, such as the ability to be creative. The list of what these two chapters can tell us is almost endless. For example, do you know that there are two different stories attributed to two different authors about how God created the world? Do you know that God created the day to start in the evening and not in the morning and that the first thing God created wasn't light but chaos?

Trailblazers

- **God**
- **Adam**
- **Eve**

These initial chapters of the Bible reveal God's creative love and imagination and God's invitation to men and women to help continue to create God's world. In the first Creation story, God speaks the world into being. God's word commands life into existence. The earth and the waters and all of the vegetation and animals were created before humans were. Creating man and woman together was God's finishing touch and the only part of Creation made in God's image. The second Creation story is where we first read about God creating Adam and Eve. God forms man out of the dust and breathes new life into being. Then God plants a garden as humankind's first home.

- What have you made that you were very proud of? What motivated you to make it?

- Have you ever handcrafted a Christmas or birthday gift for somebody? Whom? How did he or she react? How did that reaction make you feel?

2 NOW READ GENESIS 1–2.

HAPPY HUSTLERS 4H MEETING
SCHEDULE
2011

January 16, 2011	Community Meeting
February 13, 2011	Community Meeting
March 13, 2011	Community Meeting
April 10, 2011	Community Meeting
May 08, 2011	Community Meeting
June 12, 2011	Fair Sign Up (?)
July	Picnic (TBD)

3 Switchback

As you were reading through Genesis 1, did you notice the recurring phrase, "And God saw that it was good"? When God creates something, it is done so purposefully and whatever is created comes out exactly the way God desires. God looks at every aspect of Creation, sees it for what it is, and calls it good.

God thinks that human beings need one another to live faithfully and joyfully in God's created world. So God made Eve to be a partner and a helper to Adam, not to serve him as an unequal creation, but so that the two could be in community together, supporting and helping each other.

- Which Creation story do you like better? Why?

- In light of the fact that you were created by God, lovingly and on purpose, what, do you think, does God think of you?

- What does it mean to be made in the image of God?

Pace Pusher

Did you notice that when God speaks of creating humans in God's image, God uses the plural possessive *our*? (Genesis 1:26). Flip in your Bible to the Gospel of John, in the New Testament; and read John 1:1-18.

4 Prayer

Dear God, thank you for making us in your image. Teach us what that means, and help us treat others as though they are made in your image as well. Amen.

As you read through the Creation account in Genesis, you may be scratching your head, thinking that the order of things just doesn't add up. In Chapter 1, God creates land animals and human beings on the sixth day. In Chapter 2, we read that God creates humans first then land animals. What's going on here? We have been taught that dinosaurs existed for millions of years before the first humans. How can this be?

Well first, don't forget that the Bible says that God doesn't measure time the same way we do (2 Peter 3:8). Also the Bible isn't trying to be a schematic or a step-by-step set of instructions on how to create the world. The Bible's purpose isn't really to tell us *how* God created the world but *that* God created the world and everything in it, including you, lovingly and on purpose.

Fruit Trees and Fig Leaves
Genesis 3–5

1 Scouting the Terrain

Chapter 3 introduces the serpent, the first creature in opposition to God's desires for obedience, trust, peace, and loving community. We quickly learn that anything in opposition to God's desires is sin and that sin disrupts community: our relationship with God, with ourselves, with one another, and with our natural environment. The serpent knows that his question will plant seeds of doubt in Eve's mind about God's loving intentions for Creation. In answering the serpent, Eve has to repeat what she already knows—that disobeying God's word has dire consequences. As we follow the story, Adam and Eve eat the forbidden fruit but don't die a physical death immediately. What happens instead? They die to their innocence and lose their ability to be in a pure relationship with God. The story of Adam and Eve is primarily about how sin enters the world through human disobedience and lack of trust in God. But it is also a lesson about God's mercy and how God creates boundaries out of love for us. We will see God's continued mercy and care in the face of human sin in the story of Cain and Abel, the first children born to a woman.

Trailblazers

- **God**
- **Adam**
- **Eve**
- **Serpent**
- **Cain**
- **Abel**

• Have you ever been tempted to do something that you knew was wrong? What was the temptation? What did you do?

• What are some consequences that you have had to endure because you did something wrong?

• Have you ever been jealous? What made you jealous? How did you handle it?

2 NOW READ GENESIS 3–5.

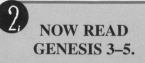

3 Switchback

There is nothing in the story of Cain and Abel that suggests why God preferred Abel's offering. So often we learn to depict Cain as wicked and devious from the start. But this might be a good example of the fact that God can do whatever God wants, without having to explain the reasons. God chose to favor Abel, and this led to conflict between the brothers. This doesn't mean that Cain's actions are excusable; but it does suggest that sometimes life is unfair, even when we do all of the things we think are right. That's a hard truth to swallow, isn't it? But some other lessons we can learn from this story are the importance of controlling our emotions and the fact that we are, indeed, our brother's and sister's keeper.

- When Adam and Eve sinned by failing to trust in God's wisdom and love, how did they react? *They were embarrased, hid themselves.*

- What parts of Creation paid the price for Adam and Eve's sin? Read carefully. *Pain in Child Birth.*

- After God punishes Adam and Eve, how does God show them that they are still loved and protected? *He clothed them and allowed them to grow their own food.*

- Why, do you think, was Cain's sacrifice not accepted by God? *It was a test of Cain's faith and persevering.*

Road Signs

- **Cherubim** (CHER-uh-BIM): These are not the chubby babies with wings. There isn't a description of a cherub in the Bible. The things we know from the Bible are that cherubim had a mix of animal and human features, they had wings, and they were always associated with God.
- **The Tree of Life:** This sacred tree was supposed to give eternal life.
- **Keeper of Sheep:** Abel's job made his lifestyle semi-nomadic. He would have had to herd sheep to different parts of the land for food, water, and protection from wild beasts.
- **Tiller of the Ground:** Cain was a farmer.
- **The Mark of Cain:** This was God's protective mark on Cain so that no one would kill him. The mark points to God's mercy even in punishment.

4 Prayer

All-Knowing God, sometimes you act in ways we don't understand; and sometimes our human response to your ways is to sin against you and against our brothers and sisters. Even though our human emotions can be used for good purposes, please teach us how to control our feelings of anger and jealousy so that we don't harm the people we should love. Amen.

Noah and the Ark
Genesis 6–9

1 Scouting the Terrain

As humanity continues in violence and rebels against God's plan for Creation, we see more of God's emotions. God grieves, is deeply saddened at humanity's violence, and regrets having made humans. Remember that we are made in God's image, so we shouldn't be surprised that God has feelings and emotions. Still, it's surprising to imagine God having regrets, isn't it? God didn't create people to be robots, programmed to do everything God commands. God created humans with hearts and the freedom to make choices, and God desires that people choose to be in relationship with God. But as we saw from the garden, humans tend to use their freedom the wrong way. God's sadness and regrets are a result of our human choices to hurt one another and to hurt our environment. But if God loves us, why would God destroy us? When we think about the story of the flood, we wonder how God could be so cruel as to destroy the whole earth—even the people who may have been innocent and the animals that had never hurt anyone. But Genesis 6:12 says, "*All* flesh had corrupted its ways upon the earth." Have you ever thought that, instead of focusing on how harsh a judgment it was for God to destroy the earth, there is something more to learn about God from the fact God spared Noah, Noah's family, and some animals—like mercy?

What three examples from days 1–3 point to God's mercy in judgment? Then go to *amazingbiblerace.com* to take a short quiz to check your research.

Trailblazers

- **God**
- **Noah**
- **Shem**
- **Ham**
- **Japheth**

• God could have totally destroyed humanity but decided to save it through Noah. What does that say about how God feels about us?

• Noah was a farmer and not a carpenter, shipbuilder, or engineer. What does that say about the people God calls on to accomplish God's work?

3 Switchback

Maybe you're starting to see a pattern of divine action. When humans sin, God judges our sin; and there are consequences. Yet, from the biblical stories we've read so far, God always seems to show mercy, even when our behavior doesn't deserve it.

God remembers Noah and blesses him with a second chance. God's blessing is an invitation for humans to reclaim their freedom and dominion in God's created world. And God even extends human boundaries by allowing them now to eat meat. The freedom God gives us is unique because it is a freedom that binds us to a certain way of life and to honor God and all God's creation.

- God sets the rainbow in the sky as a sign of the covenant God made with Noah. Who or what else was included in the covenant?

- What does Noah do first after leaving the ark? Have you ever paused to give thanks to God after coming out of a very hard time?

- The Scripture says that God spared Noah because he was the only one righteous before God. What phrase appears repeatedly in today's reading that emphasizes Noah's relationship with God?

2 NOW READ GENESIS 6–9.

Road Signs

- **Nephilim (NEF-uh-lim):** These are giants born from the inter-mingling of human females and divine male creatures. Such unions symbolized increasing chaos on earth.
- **Cypress wood:** This is a slow-growing, coniferous tree that is extremely resistant to decay and insects; it can be more than 100-feet high or a simple shrub.
- **Pitch:** This natural adhesive in the form of a gummy, black substance is extracted from trees.
- **Cubit:** This is an ancient measuring term. One cubit equals the distance from the elbow to the tip of one's middle finger.

4 Prayer

Merciful God, you see and know the innermost parts of our hearts. Forgive us when our thoughts and actions cause you to grieve in your own heart. And help us use our freedom to care for people and the natural world. Amen.

The Tower of Babel
Genesis 10–11

1 Scouting the Terrain

Trailblazers

- Shem
- Ham
- Japheth
- Their descendants

The whole earth is repopulated from Noah's three sons: Shem, Ham and Japheth. But even with this new population some things remain the same. Humans remain eager to cross the boundaries that God has established for them. The story of the Tower of Babel is one more story about people not trusting God and wanting to secure their own futures and lives by their own means and wisdom. Notice the guiding force behind the people's desire to build a tower to the heavens: pride and fear.

Pay attention as the biblical narrative continues. Pride and fear will continue to be two of the chief reasons that humans choose to disobey God and to act from lack of trust in God's word and God's provision.

But God, who always desires to be part of our hopes and plans, comes down from above to see what the people are up to and finds them once again plotting to determine their own rules for living in the world. So God gives everyone new and different languages so that nobody understands anyone else and God does the very thing that people feared, scatters them throughout the earth. The self-devised plan of the people backfires.

WEEK

1
◈
DAY

4

- Have you ever been part of a team that worked very well together and seemed to be invincible? If so, to what did you credit your team's success?

- Have you ever felt as though you could make it on your own, without God's help?

2 NOW READ GENESIS 10–11.

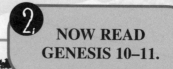

3 Switchback

Genesis 11:10 is the beginning of a significant part of the biblical story. It traces the family line of Abram and tells some interesting family tidbits about the man whom God would choose to become the father of the Israelite people, affecting the future of the entire world population.

We all know that no family is perfect and that every family has one or two skeletons in its closet, or that some sad and unfortunate fate has befallen a member of the family. Abram's family is no different. Haran, Abram's brother, dies before his time, leaving his father a grieving man with the misfortune of mourning a son. In those days, it was considered extremely bad luck for a son to die before a father. On top of that, Abram's wife, Sarai, couldn't have any children. Being a mother was considered a symbol of God's blessing and a source of pride. As a barren woman, other women would have looked down on Sarai.

- Why, do you think, was God concerned about humans all speaking the same language?

- Which of Noah's sons could boast of having the first warrior in history as a descendant?

- How is Genesis 11 a contrasting story of Genesis 10? What is the phenomenon that both chapters are trying to explain?

4 Prayer

God of heaven and earth, help us seek to catch your attention by doing things to glorify you and not by doing things out of fear and pride. Amen.

Road Signs

- **Babel** (BAY-buhl): This is a play on words and meaning. It is the Hebrew name for Babylon, an ancient Mesopotamian city, which also means "the gate of God." But in Hebrew, the verb meaning "to confuse" is *balal,* very similar to *Babel.*
- **Ur of the Chaldeans:** This was Abraham's home of origin.

Abram and Sarai
Genesis 12–15

1) Scouting the Terrain

The most significant thing we know about Abram up till now is that his wife, Sarai, can't have children. Who will care for Abram and Sarai in their old age? Who will continue Noah's family line and the repopulation of the Earth? Haran, his brother, is already dead; and at the end of Chapter 11, we are left with the bleak picture of a dwindling family with a newly deceased grandfather Terah.

Trailblazers

- **God**
- **Abram**
- **Sarai**
- **Lot**

Then God enters the scene with a word, a call, and a promise for new life and a new future. The call of Abram is God giving humanity yet another chance at living faithfully by God's standards. Through Abram God seeks to create a new people, a new nation, and an even more intense level of interaction between humanity and God. To begin this new relationship with God, Abram must learn to let go of the life he knew and trust God's word. God asks Abram to give up three sets of things: his sense of home and belonging, his community and family, and his comfort and stability. No one ever said obeying God was easy. Sometimes following God is not about being safe, secure, and comfortable, but about taking risks and starting new journeys. How does Abram respond? The Bible doesn't say anything about complaints or bargaining with God. Instead, it says, "Abram went, as the LORD had told him." Abram chose to blindly trust God.

• Whom do you know who you would say is a faithful follower of God?

• Do you know someone who has given up much in pursuit of God's will?

• Why, do you think, was Abram so quick to respond to God's requests?

fast forward Walk a labyrinth and reflect on a time when you felt that being faithful to God meant being uncomfortable, scared, and uncertain about the future. What sorts of things, thoughts, or people helped you make a decision? (Be sure to photograph or video your group in the labyrinth to upload at *amazingbiblerace.com*. Or post a blog reflection about the experience, instead.)

2 NOW READ GENESIS 12–15.

3 Switchback

Abram left his home, as God asked. And while that was a faithful move, he has already acted very human by making Sarai pose as his sister, potentially putting her in danger, just to save his own skin from Pharaoh. So when God appears again, Abram is less willing to obey without question. He points out the obvious to God, "What will you give me, for I continue childless?" and simply questions God's ability to do all that God promises, regardless of the circumstances. God's reply is a reminder to Abram, and us as the readers, that when God promises to provide, we should never imagine that it will be second best. Abram's child will be of his own flesh and blood. With that issue settled, Abram now wants proof that God will also keep the promise about giving him some land. So God, who never has to prove anything to us, willingly enters into an old-fashioned contract with Abram. Yet this covenant with Abram was more like a gift than a contract. Abram doesn't have to do anything to receive all that God has now promised him, or does he?

• What is it about Abram and Sarai's life that makes them think that God's promises sound especially ridiculous? Do you suppose they believed that these promises would come true?

Road Signs

• **Covenant:** This is an agreement between two parties. The ancient custom of making a covenant was to cut animals in half and then have each group or person from both sides of the agreement walk through the animals. This was a way of saying that if either party didn't keep their end of the bargain they were willing to become like the dead, halved animals.

• **Canaanites** (KAY-nuh-nights): These are people of Canaan, from whom God would take their land and give it to the Hebrew people as their Promised Land. Today Canaan covers parts of Israel and Lebanon.

• **Bethel:** This is a town located on the road to Jerusalem.

• **Pharaoh:** (FAYR-oh): This is the Hebrew word for the king of Egypt.

• **Sodom** (SOD-uhm): Where Lot chose to live, Sodom is famous for being the sinful city where people had no regard for God and were hostile to strangers.

4 Prayer

Generous God, you offer us so many blessings. All you ask in return is our faith. Give us faith enough to let you interrupt our comfortable lives with your new visions and plans. Help us go and trust as easily as Abram did. Amen.

They Thought
They Had It Maid
Genesis 16–19

① Scouting the Terrain

Last time we saw old Abe, he was at the blessed receiving end of a covenant with God, asked to do nothing but trust and have faith. But Genesis 16:2 says, "And Abram listened to the voice of Sarai." What was Sarai saying? She told Abram that, because she was unable to have children, he should be intimate with Hagar, the maidservant. This way, when she became pregnant, they would have fulfilled God's promise. However, it's not up to people to fulfill God's promises. God fulfills God's promises. Because of this scheme, Abram, Sarai, and Hagar become mixed up in insensitivity, jealousy, and pride. Folks continue to act normally, listening to God one minute, turning a deaf ear the next, and making a mess of things.

The story of Abram, Sarai, and Hagar teaches us an increasingly familiar lesson: When we interfere with God's purposes, people get hurt and things never work out the way we want. For the most part, the chapters following Genesis 12 center on Abraham getting that promised heir somehow or another. But these four chapters, 16–19, also have some new lessons to teach us about God's love and care for us—even when we don't seek out God—about how a relationship with God changes our identity, about hospitality to strangers, about expecting God in ordinary places, and about God's willingness to engage people like friends and openness to hearing our thoughts and considerations.

Trailblazers

• **God**
• **Abraham** (formerly known as Abram)
• **Sarah** (formerly known as Sarai)
• **Hagar** (maidservant of Sarah)
• **Ishmael** (son of Abraham and Hagar)
• **Isaac** (son of Abraham and Sarah)
• **Lot**
• **Lot's Wife**

• What do you think about Sarai and Abram's Hagar scheme? Does it show a mistrust in and lack of love for God, or were they just trying to help?

• Why, do you think, did they come up with this scheme? Did they think that God's power was limited to human possibilities? How do we sometimes think that way?

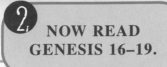

2 **NOW READ GENESIS 16–19.**

3 **Switchback**

The story of Sodom and Gomorrah is full of details about God's character and human behavior. God appears to Abraham and Sarah and promises to give them new life. Then God visits Lot and promises to take away lives. This is not the first time we've encountered a God who creates and destroys. Abraham boldly and creatively intercedes for the innocent people of Sodom. We can learn from Abe's example and courageously come before God for the sake of people who need our prayers. God may not be standing in front of us like God was with Abraham, but we know that God hears our prayers.

• When Lot and his wife were about to flee, they were told not to look back. Lot didn't, but his wife did and turned into a pillar of salt. Have you ever been through a bad situation in which it did more harm to look back than to look ahead?

4 **Prayer**

Giving Lord, teach us how to welcome strangers with kindness—providing for their needs as we are able—and how to care with generous hearts for those in our own families. Amen.

Road Signs

• **Hagar:** She was Sarai's maidservant. Back in Old Testament times, it was perfectly acceptable for a woman to offer her maid to her husband to use as a surrogate mother.
• **El-Roi:** This ancient Hebrew term meaning "God who sees." "El" means "God." God saw Hagar's desperate condition and came to her rescue. In ancient times, God was considered such an awesome force that people believed that beholding, or seeing, God was enough to kill a person.
• **El-Shaddai** (EL SHAD-igh): This Hebrew name for God means "God Almighty."
• **Abraham:** This name means "Father of Multitudes."
• **Circumcision:** This is the Hebrew practice of removing the foreskin from the penis as a sign of God's covenant with the Abraham and all of his descendants.

Father Abraham
Genesis 20–23

1 Scouting the Terrain

Sometimes fear causes us to do regrettable things, such as striking out with violence, hurtful words, or lies. Sarah is a beautiful woman; and she catches the eye of Abimelech, the king of a foreign land that she and Abraham wandered into. Fearing that the king will have Abraham killed so that he can take her for his own wife, Abraham lies and tells everybody that Sarah is his sister.

So the king takes Sarah, intending to be intimate with her. But before he does, God speaks to Abimelech in a dream and sets the story straight. This interaction between God and Abimelech reminds us that God has relationships with people outside of the Abrahamic covenant, and sometimes those people show more faith than God's chosen people do. Abraham's lying was based out of fear for his own life and not out of trust in God. But out of God's grace, God still uses Abraham, reminding us that God's faithfulness to us stems from God's love and God's own desires. Rarely is it dependent on our obedience and faithfulness to God.

Trailblazers

- **God**
- **Abraham**
- **Sarah**
- **Abimelech**
  (king of Negreb)
- **Isaac**
- **Hagar**
- **Ishmael**

Finally, Sarah has her baby, just as God had promised. It is truly a miracle because God brought new life from a practically dead womb. The things that are impossible by human standards are always possible with God. Just like when the Spirit of God raised Jesus from the dead. Nothing is impossible for God. Sarah is so overwhelmed by this birth that all she can do is laugh. There are no words to explain it. She and Abraham name the child Isaac.

- Has fear ever motivated you to do something regrettable? What happened?

- When has it been easier to lie than to tell the truth?

2.

NOW READ
GENESIS 20–23.

3. Switchback

Genesis 22 is one of the best-known passages of the Old Testament. It is the difficult and incomprehensible story of God's testing of Abraham and providing for Abraham. It is hard to imagine a God that would ask someone to sacrifice his or her only child. God doesn't even give Abraham a reason. We, the readers, know that it is a test; but poor Abraham doesn't know that. All he knows is that God has called him to take his only child, the child he has waited for all his life, the child that God promised him, somewhere to kill him. This experience must have revealed to Abraham a new side of God. Abraham realizes a little more what it means to have faith and what it means to serve the Almighty God, Creator of heaven and earth.

Road Signs

• **Beer-sheba** (BEE-uhr-SHEE-buh): This is the site of the covenant between Abimelech and Abraham and is where Abraham builds another altar.

There are many things to reflect on in this hard passage: Abraham's complaint-free and swift obedience; God's testing of human being; Abraham's hope and faith that somehow God would handle this situation, rather than his hoping for a specific outcome at the end of this ordeal; the story's suggestion that God didn't know how much Abraham loved God and the extent of Abraham's trust and faith; and, of course, wonderment at what Isaac thought and felt throughout all of this. It is easy to imagine that this was a traumatic and life-changing experience for everyone.

Directly following this narrative is the story of Sarah's death, and after this event there is no more recorded conversation between Abraham and God.

• When has God called you to do something and you acted obediently?

• Why, do you think, would God ask such a great thing of Abraham?

4. Prayer

Almighty God, give us the strength to do all you command of us, even when we don't understand your ways. Amen.

Double Trouble
Genesis 24–26

1 Scouting the Terrain

After demanding Isaac's life and then giving it back to him, God now provides a suitable wife for Isaac. In a way, Isaac has been given a new lease on life; and the next section of the Genesis narrative focuses on his newly created family. Perhaps a special relationship also existed between God and Isaac. God blesses him with material wealth; and, when Isaac prays for his barren wife, God blesses him twofold, having Rebekah become pregnant with twins. But even before the twins are born, the family drama begins. God simply tells Rebekah that her sons will be rivals and that relationships will not develop as she may hope. Jacob and Esau are born, Isaac and Rebekah have favorites, and immediately we begin to see the differences in the personality of the boys. The twins' struggle in Rebekah's womb also sets the stage for the long list of family struggles and rivalries that will plague Isaac and Rebekah's descendants. This is another example of God's seemingly random election. God chooses Jacob to rule over Esau. If that's true, then can we really blame Jacob and Esau for their actions? That's a hard question with no easy answer. Esau continues to make poor choices. This section ends with him marrying a non-Hebrew and making his parents miserable.

Trailblazers

- **God**
- **Abraham**
- **Isaac**
- **Rebekah** (Isaac's wife)
- **Abraham's servant**
- **Jacob and Esau** (twin sons of Isaac and Rebekah)

• Do you have a rival? If so, what makes your relationship with this person so contentious?

• When was the last time you thought that your parents were being unfair? What happened?

2 NOW READ GENESIS 24–26.

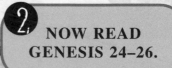

22

3 Switchback

God reaffirms the covenant with Isaac and lets him know that it's because of Abraham's faithfulness that the promise is passed down. Notice how God chooses to self-identify to Isaac, "I am the God of your father Abraham; do not be afraid, for I am with you." This tells Isaac, and us, that God isn't just any old god. This is a specific god, the God of Abraham, the God who enters into relationships with people and has expectations of people. God exists in family history; God keeps promises.

• What does it mean to you that this God, the God of Abraham and Isaac, is your God too?

Road Signs

• **Birthright:** This is the tradition that the eldest son is heir to twice as much of his father's inheritance.
• **Hand under the thigh:** This was an ancient way of making a promise to someone.
• **Shekel:** The standard for measurement of weight that is equivalent to about 14 grams of silver.

4 Prayer

Lord, help us to recognize the gifts you give us and keep us from foolishly squandering our blessings. Amen.

 One way in which names were significant in the Hebrew culture is that they identified how God related to people. Make a list of the names of Jacob's sons and, based on the narrative, write out the definition of each son's name. Then go to *amazingbiblerace.com* to take a short quiz to check your research.

Deception
Genesis 27–30

1 Scouting the Terrain

Jacob is really a man of trickery and deceit. Not only does he cheat Esau out of his birthright, but he also has no qualms about lying to and deceiving his aging father, Isaac, and stealing his brother's rightful blessing. Jacob even lies in the name of God. But still, of all people, Jacob is chosen by, visited by, and blessed by God.

Jacob's first encounter with God, where God passes on the covenant to him, is in the middle of his escape journey from Esau's anger and on his quest to find a suitable wife. Jacob does not consider his place of rest anything special. It is merely somewhere for him to take a break in between his old home and his future destination. In fact, he is surprised to discover God's presence in such a seemingly ordinary place.

God comes to Jacob. This seems to be one of the consistent ways that God appears to people. The details of the dream are pretty significant. One interpretation of Jacob's ladder is that it symbolizes God's constant interaction with his creatures on earth. The angels traveling back and forth between heaven and earth suggest that even though we may not know it, God is always at work in our lives.

- Have you ever been the victim of a deception? What happened? How did it make you feel? How did you respond?

Trailblazers

- **God**
- **Isaac**
- **Rebekah**
- **Jacob**
- **Esau**
- **Laban** (father of Rachel and Leah)
- **Leah**
- **Rachel** (Leah's younger sister)
- **Joseph** (son of Jacob and Rachel)
- **Bilhah** (Rachel's maid)
- **Zilpah** (Leah's maid)

WEEK
2
◇
DAY
4

2 NOW READ GENESIS 27–30.

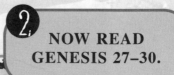

3 Switchback

Trouble seems to follow the wily Jacob wherever he goes. Laban, his future father-in-law, gives Jacob a taste of his own medicine, tricking him into marrying Leah after having him work seven years for Rachel's hand and then having him work an additional seven years for Rachel.

Poor Leah! Not only is her younger sister Rachel prettier than she is, but she's also more desired by Jacob. But thankfully, God remembers all of God's children—even those who get slighted by others. Leah has her first son, Reuben; and then eventually, with Leah, Rachel, Bilhah, and Zilpah, Jacob fathers twelve sons and one daughter. The descendants of these twelve sons form the twelve tribes of Israel. After Joseph, the eleventh son, is born, Jacob is ready to continue his journey. In conning Laban out of much of his livestock, Jacob skillfully manages to repay Laban for the bridal deceit and having had to work fourteen years for Rachel.

- What do you think about the fact God chose to visit and bless someone like Jacob? Does that seem right? Why, or why not?

- God visits Jacob in what seems to be an ordinary place. What are some ordinary places in your life where you'd be surprised to experience God's presence?

Road Signs

- **Oil poured over the pillar:** Oil was used in religious rites to symbolize holiness unto God.
- **Mandrakes:** This plant was often used for its medicinal purposes and was believed to help women conceive. It has greenish-yellow flowers and a branched root that resembles the human body. The fruit of the plant is the May apple.
- **Divination:** This is one way in which humans tried to find out God's purposes or to appeal to the gods to act on their behalf.

4 Prayer

Thank you, God, that in your mercy and grace you visit us and care for us in all circumstances; when we feel forgotten by others in our lives and even when our actions fail to mirror your loving and honest ways. Amen.

Time to Face the Music
Genesis 31–34

① Scouting the Terrain

The final confrontation between these two swindlers comes after Jacob flees with his family and possessions. When Jacob's wealth begins to pose a threat to Laban's family God tells him to return home. During Laban's pursuit of Jacob God also appears to Laban in a dream and warns him against harming Jacob. God's presence and protection are constantly with Jacob and Laban is forced to recognize the God of Abraham, Isaac, and Jacob and acknowledges his defeat. He saves face by suggesting that he and Jacob make a covenant before God as a witness.

With one confrontation behind him, Jacob prepares for the next one, meeting his brother, Esau. In Jacob-like fashion, he plots ways to appease Esau's anger in case Esau still wants to kill him after all these years. It's one of the first times we see Jacob anxious and worried. What if his craftiness can't get him out of this one? He also calls on God, reminding God of the covenant and of God's promise to be with him. And God remains faithful to Jacob.

Trailblazers

- **God**
- **Jacob** (also known as **Israel)**
- **Laban**
- **Rachel**
- **Leah**
- **Esau**
- **Dinah** (Jacob's daughter)
- **Simeon and Levi** (Jacob's sons)

- Have you ever had to "face the music" with someone you have wronged? What happened?

- How has God shown faithfulness to you during a time of need?

Road Signs

- **Mizpah:** (MIZ-puh) This is the Hebrew word for "watchtower." The covenant between Laban and Jacob is known as the "Mizpah Benediction" because Laban prayed that God would keep watch over their pact.
- **Household gods:** These idols were believed to secure family leadership and property.
- **"The way of women is upon me.":** Rachel was referring to her menstrual cycle.
- **Peniel** (PEN-ee-uhl)**:** This is the Hebrew word for "face of God."

2. NOW READ GENESIS 31–34.

3 Switchback

On the eve of his meeting with Esau, Jacob intends to spend a solemn night alone; but he ends up wrestling with God all night long. It's hard to know why Jacob encounters God in this way and why he seems able to hold his own in a wrestling match with God. We know from previous chapters that Jacob is a man of incredible strength. Remember when he first sees Rachel, in Chapter 29; and he moves the stone from the well by himself? But that still doesn't tell us how "the man ... did not prevail against Jacob." Perhaps Jacob's deep longing for a divine blessing on this night before meeting Esau was so great that it empowered him to cling tight to God until God did indeed bless him. Whatever the reason, one thing is certain: Humans rarely have such intimate encounters with God without something to show for it. Jacob is left with a limp to remind him of his struggle with God and with a divine name change to symbolize his new identity as one who fights with both God and humans.

• Do you think that people still "wrestle with God" today? In what ways?

• The meeting between Jacob and Esau is full of polite and respectful exchanges. Gifts are offered back and forth, and the two brothers act as though their shared history is forgotten. Does this sound realistic? Why, or why not?

• What happens at the end of the story that suggests that the two brothers are merely being guarded with each other, both well aware of their tainted past?

4 Prayer

Lord, we thank you that, even in our struggles with you, you still mercifully bless us. Help us bear the marks of our encounters with you. Amen.

Water Break

Congratulations on completing another week of the race. You're already more than halfway through the first book of the Bible. By now, you may have begun to appreciate, and maybe even identify with, the struggles and shortcomings of some of our biblical heroes. Isn't it comforting to know that, despite these persons' imperfections, God continues to love them and bless them? Isn't it great to know that the same is true for us?

Joseph the Dreamer
Genesis 35–37

1 Scouting the Terrain

After the rape of Dinah and the retaliatory violence perpetrated by Levi and Simeon, a new chapter in Jacob's life begins. God reaches out to him and, amidst further instructions, God changes Jacob's name to Israel. (The Scriptural text will alternate back and forth, referring to him as both Jacob and Israel.) God redirects Jacob to Bethel, the place where Jacob had his first encounter with God. The narrative highlights a shift in Jacob's faith life. He makes all who are traveling with him get rid of their foreign gods; and he erects an altar to God, as God has demanded of him. This symbolizes Jacob's heightened commitment to following the God of Abraham and Isaac and doing everything possible to remain clean of other cultural influences that threaten worship of God.

Notice a pattern when people encounter God, whether God speaks or appears in some form, that the human response is always worship. And God always honors the promises made to those who worship God. Jacob is the last individual of the Bible who will bear God's three-fold covenant promise. From now on it will be a promise God will repeatedly speak to the Israelites who now consist of the twelve sons of Jacob but will eventually become a nation of people. Abraham, Isaac, and Jacob are considered the patriarchs (fathers) of the Israelite nation.

- Have you ever made some big changes in order to recommit yourself to God?

- What are some things that you might change in your life in order to walk more closely with God?

Racing Tip

To tear one's clothing and wear sackcloth was a sign of deep mourning.

Trailblazers

- **God**
- **Jacob** (a.k.a. **Israel**)
- **Joseph**

2 NOW READ GENESIS 35–37.

28

3 Switchback

Chapter 37 begins a new story, that of Jacob's son Joseph. His story of betrayal, kidnapping, apparent good fortune, imprisonment, and rise to power bears lasting significance for the future of Israel. As the tale begins, we could fault Joseph for being an attention-seeker and a braggart, sharing his grandiose dreams with his brothers. But Joseph was also a courageous person. He acknowledged his God-given gift to dream vividly, and he shared his dreams in honest sincerity. Perhaps he could have done a little more to calm his brothers in their heated response. But it still often takes courage for us to speak our dreams aloud. What if the dreams don't come true or other people are offended and feel threatened by our dreams, as Joseph's brothers were?

Notice that God doesn't speak directly to Joseph but speaks through nightly visions, the way God appeared to his father, Jacob. Even though God seems absent in these new stories compared to God's speaking and revealing himself in the lives of Abraham, Isaac, and Jacob, God is still at work behind the scenes.

• Do you have any dreams that might require courage to speak them aloud?

• Can you think of a time when God was at work behind the scenes in your life and you didn't realize exactly how until much later?

Road Signs

• **Terror of God:** This is fear of the divine.
• **Ben-oni:** This name means 'Son of my sorrow."
• **Benjamin:** This name means "son of power."
• **concubine** (KON-kyew-bighn)**:** This pseudo-wife is a woman who would live in a man's house and would have sexual relations with him but would not have authority in the family, as a wife would.
• **Ishmaelites:** These are the descendants of Ishmael, Abraham's first son and Isaac's half-brother.
• **Cistern:** This is a hole where water is stored.
• **Edom:** This is the land where the descendants of Esau lived.
• **Sheaves:** These are tied-up bundles of cut stalks of grain.
• **Sheol** (SHEE-ohl)**:** This is the dark, silent place where people of Bible times believed they would go after they died, a place where they would no longer exist.

4 Prayer

Dear God, please give us the courage to speak our dreams aloud to others. And help us encourage other people in fulfilling their dreams. Amen.

The Tale of Tamar
Genesis 38–41

① Scouting the Terrain

A story with a woman at the center, the tale of Tamar is about a woman using her limited resources to seek out the justice she deserves. Tamar is one of few women mentioned in Scripture as playing a role in Jesus' ancestry. In those days it was the custom for the next son in birth order to fill the role of providing an heir to the family if the first son dies. That usually meant fathering the child of a sister-in-law. A woman's future depended on the men in her life; and if Tamar was without a husband or a son, she would be at a loss for livelihood. Neither Er nor Onan took the responsibilities they should have; and Judah did not want to risk the death of his third son, since the other two sons died while in Tamar's company. So Tamar had to use her intelligence to secure her future.

Road Signs

- **Cupbearer:** This is the person who served Pharaoh his wine. This was considered an important position.

Trailblazers

- **God**
- **Judah** (son of Jacob)
- **Shuah** (wife of Judah)
- **Er, Onan, and Shelah** (sons of Judah and Shuah)
- **Tamar** (wife of Er)
- **Joseph**
- **Potiphar** (captain of the Pharaoh's guard, who takes Joseph into his house)
- **Pharaoh's cupbearer and chief baker**

So what can we learn from this story? Even though God is not mentioned in the tale, we can assume that God is a God of justice; and because Tamar's actions led to the birth of Perez, of whom Jesus is a descendant, we can also assume that God blessed Tamar's actions. God wants women to be treated justly, and God uses women as well as men to carry out the divine plan for humanity.

- Look back at the stories you've read so far. What other women has God used directly or indirectly to play a role in the overall story of God's promise to the Abraham and his descendants?

② NOW READ GENESIS 38–41.

3 Switchback

After a brief literary interlude, we return to the story of Joseph and finally get to hear what has happened to him. Well, God is with the dreamer. God protects Joseph's life and is with him through the good times and the bad times. Joseph's life seems a roller coaster ride of ups and downs. First, he's bought by an Egyptian of social and political status who makes him head of his household affairs; then he's framed and wrongfully imprisoned. But through it all Joseph continues to use his gifts to witness for God, even in times of adversity. When he has the chance to interpret dreams for his fellow prisoners, he begins by acknowledging that God is the ultimate dream interpreter, thereby attributing his gifts to God's provision. As a result of Joseph's faithful use of his gifts, he is eventually released from prison and brought to live and serve in a prominent position in the Pharaoh's house. Again, while God is acting behind the scenes, it takes human effort and faithful living to bring about God's good intentions for us.

• According to this story, does God's timing always match ours?

• Where is an example of Joseph having to be patient and trust that God will not forget him in his difficult times?

• One of the many ways God comes to us is by speaking and acting through other people. We see that in the story of Joseph and Pharaoh, especially. Have you ever experienced God through another person?

Weekly Challenge

Remember how we talked about the importance of names and how they suggest a person's relationship or feelings toward God? Read through the story of Joseph in Egypt. When Joseph becomes second in command over Egypt and establishes his own family, how does he immortalize God's actions in his past and present? Then go to *amazingbiblerace.com* to take a short quiz to check your research.

4 Prayer

Dear Lord, help us use our gifts to witness to others about your abilities. Amen.

I Thought He Looked Familiar
Genesis 42–45

1 Scouting the Terrain

In these emotionally charged chapters, Joseph and his brothers are reunited; and Joseph has the upper hand because they don't recognize him. We might imagine this as the perfect time for revenge, but Joseph doesn't seem as interested in revenge as we might be. Instead, he puts his brothers through a series of tests—to find out whether they've changed; perhaps to remind them subtly of their betrayal; to find out information about his father and younger brother, Benjamin; and then perhaps to decide what to do next with the ten brothers. From an examination of Joseph's emotions, we can tell that he is still hurt by his brothers' betrayal and is still longing for his family. As for his brothers, they are going through their own feelings of guilt and perhaps remorse. They think that God is punishing them for what they did to Joseph.

Trailblazers

- Joseph
- Joseph's brothers
- Jacob

This is a beautiful but sad story of family drama, the relationship between brothers, the choice of whether to seek revenge or forgiveness, the longing for home, and the desire to correct old mistakes. There are no easy answers, and the narrative does a good job of reminding us that people of faith are not perfect but often lead messy lives. God's presence does not mean that life will be easy. We've seen that in all of the biblical stories so far. As people of faith, we still have to work at forgiveness and confession and at doing the right thing in God's eyes.

- Can you think of a time in your life when a really good thing came out of a really bad experience?

- How was God at work?

2 NOW READ GENESIS 42–45.

3 Switchback

The idea that God is at work in the brothers' betrayal of Joseph is hard to swallow. Would God sell someone into slavery or make someone endure being kidnapped for the sake of God's grand plan for humanity? That's hard to imagine. Not only does that make God sound unloving, but it also takes the blame off the brothers for their wicked actions. A different take on the situation might be that Joseph's brothers used their God-given human freedom to make decisions and chose to act sinfully. But out of God's love and because all things are possible with God, God can still bring about good despite human sinful choices. God would rather have humans cooperate for the good of the world, but so often we fail to be God's faithful partners in seeking healing and peace.

• How is Joseph's treatment of his brothers representative of both our human struggle to forgive and forget and our human faithfulness to God's love?

• Does this story about a biblical family make you think something different or new about how your family lives and loves together?

• How do you try to cooperate with God to bring about healing and peace in your community?

4 Prayer

Healing God, we know that we don't have to hear your voice to recognize your work in our lives. Help us learn to be more forgiving of those who hurt us and more interested in rebuilding relationships than in seeking revenge. Amen.

Jacob in Egypt
Genesis 46–48

WEEK
3
◆
DAY
4

1 Scouting the Terrain

God remains faithfully with Jacob. Israel, in the form of Jacob and his descendants, moves from Canaan to Egypt. On the way out of town, Jacob stops to worship God; and God affirms and blesses the journey. This is a significant move for the future of the nation of Israel that will turn out to be part of how God will fulfill God's promises to Abraham, Isaac, and Jacob. And as soon they enter Egypt, we get a hint of the present and future relationship between the Egyptian and Hebrew people. Jacob and his family will be permitted to stay because of Joseph's favorable relationship with Pharaoh, but they will still have to live on the outskirts of town in a place called Goshen.

Trailblazers

- **Jacob and sons**
- **Joseph**
- **Manasseh and Ephraim** (Joseph's sons)

Another hint of the relationship between the two ethnic groups is based on the Egyptian people's economic dependence on Joseph, a foreigner in their midst who now has control of the land and the food supply. He does all this to secure stability and to enable everyone to be fed, but the Egyptians in years to come will not always look so thankfully toward those of Hebrew ancestry. These tidbits to the story help us prepare for the plot of the next book, Exodus.

- Can you think of a time when you stopped to worship God before embarking on some new challenge in your life?

- When might it be an appropriate time for you to do so?

- By now you have read almost all of Genesis. What do you recall were God's promises to Abraham, Isaac, and Jacob?

2 NOW READ GENESIS 46–48.

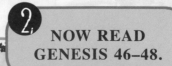

③ Switchback

Just before Jacob dies, he passes on God's covenantal promises to his son Joseph; and he blesses Joseph's two sons, Manasseh and Ephraim. Jacob's blessing to Joseph reveals crucial aspects of God's identity and how God has factored into the lives of Joseph's ancestors.

First, Jacob acknowledges God as the one who was present before Abraham and Isaac. This is a God with a history of being faithfully present with Jacob's family. Then Jacob describes God as a shepherd, the one who guided and protected Jacob all of his life. Finally, Jacob describes God as an angel who saves his life. Obviously there are many more ways that Jacob could have described God but he picks descriptions that stem from important aspects of his personal life experience. He was a shepherd by trade so he knows what qualities make a good shepherd. He knows firsthand how God acts in people's lives, and he has experienced God as an angel with whom he wrestled and from whom he received a blessing.

• Based on some of your own personal life experiences, what are three ways that you would describe God?

• Even though Jacob's life was richly blessed by God would you say Jacob had an easy life? Why?

④ Prayer

Generous God, sometimes your blessings are difficult to see because we have our human hearts set on our own desires. Help us to see the many ways you bless us even in the midst of challenges and trials. Amen.

The Death of Jacob
Genesis 49–50

WEEK
3
◈
DAY
5

1 Scouting the Terrain

The saga of the Genesis families comes to a dramatic end. Jacob is about to die so he blesses his sons as was the custom. In Jacob's blessings we read about the fate of his sons but also about the future of the 12 tribes of Israel, of which each son represents one. The blessings reveal a mixture of outcomes, positive, negative, and undetermined. Like most families this biblical family is made up of people with a variety of temperaments and personalities. In fact, Jacob likens a number of his sons to animals that represent certain characteristics. Judah is like a lion, Issachar is like a donkey, and Naphtali is like a doe. But God will still use these people and their descendants to bless the world. God uses God's children despite our many human flaws and interesting personalities. Think about how God used Joseph's brothers to bring the Israelites to Egypt despite their sometimes less than perfect ways! Even Joseph recognizes that sometimes God redeems our sinful actions to effect good things in other people's lives. Now that is a gracious God!

Trailblazers

- Jacob
- Joseph and his brothers

Road Signs

- **Embalming:** This was the Egyptian custom of preparing the dead for the afterlife. It involves taking out all the internal organs and filling the body with a special preserving agent.

- Think of your family. Can you see a variety of personalities? What is one unique thing that each member brings to your family?

- What is one way you think God has used you unique to who you are?

- Just for fun, to what animal would you liken yourself? Why?

2 NOW READ GENESIS 49–50.

3 Switchback

As soon as Jacob dies, the brothers begin to worry that Joseph will seek revenge for their past sins. They focus on how to get out of potential trouble with Joseph and decide to lie to him. Some people never change, huh? But Joseph is a man of God, and he forgives his brothers. He also teaches his brothers a good lesson about God's grace. God used the wicked actions of the brothers to bring Joseph to a position of wealth and status. But the point of Joseph's position was not merely for his own benefit; it was to benefit the larger community of Egyptians and Israelites!

The Book of Genesis ends with Joseph passing on the promises of God to the Israelites. And by the time Joseph dies, the family has increased by three generations. That's a lot more Israelites than before. But this shows that God's promises are coming true; the people are multiplying from the child born of Sarah's old womb. The fulfillment of promise continues as we step out of Genesis and into Exodus.

• What are some of the ways that Joseph's initial misfortune was redeemed into benefiting the people and larger communities he encountered?

4 Prayer

Thank you God, you even work to save us and heal us when other people seek to hurt us. Help us reflect your grace by offering forgiveness to those who do hurt us. Amen.

Water Break

You have just finished the first book of the Bible! Congratulations! Wasn't it more exciting and fun to read than you anticipated? You actually learned a lot of new things about the amazing ways of God and the beauty of Creation. Now press on to the second book, Exodus.

Moses
Exodus 1–4

1 Scouting the Terrain

The story of Moses is a continuation of God's plan for fulfilling a threefold promise. Moses' survival sets the stage for Pharaoh's increasingly cruel injustice toward the Israelites. The story plays out in the Israelites' alternating response of trust and doubt in God.

In the Exodus story, a lot of people are afraid of one thing or another; and they respond to their fears in a variety of ways. Exodus is a story about learning to trust and obey God, despite our fears, our feelings of inadequacy, and the impossibility of a given situation. It also teaches us that when God calls us, God enables us to do God's work. God calls Moses, despite all Moses' excuses, and equips him for ministry.

Trailblazers

- **God**
- **Moses**
- **Pharaoh** (the ruler of Egypt)
- **Aaron** (Moses' brother)

- Has God ever called on you to do something difficult? What was it? What happened?

- Have you ever taken on a task that you knew you weren't qualified for? What happened?

- God keeps identifying God's self as "the God of your Father, Abraham, Isaac and Jacob." Why, do you think, is that?

Road Signs

- **Papyrus:** This water plant is found in the shallow parts of the Nile. Papyrus was used to make paper as well as fuel, food, clothes, medicine, and other items.
- **Bitumen:** This flammable substance occurs naturally and by distilling coal or petroleum and is used to waterproof.
- **Pitch:** This thick, dark, sticky substance is distilled from petroleum or from coal or wood tar and is used to waterproof.
- **Midian:** (MID-ee-uhn) He was the son of Abraham and Keturah. The region of Midian was in the East, and Midianites were nomadic peoples who lived primarily in the Arabian and Syrian deserts.
- **Leprosy:** This contagious disease is characterized by ulcers of the skin, bones, and intestines.

2. NOW READ EXODUS 1–4.

3. Switchback

The episode of the "burning bush" is a good example of how God appears in the midst of people going about their everyday lives, doing the normal, sometimes boring things they have to do.

Moses is minding his own business, doing his work when God interrupts him. We could focus on many details of this story, but three really stand out: First, this story suggests that wherever God is present is holy ground. Second, Moses' immediate response to God is reverent fear and awe of God. Instead of screaming in disbelief or wondering whether he is dreaming, Moses seems to readily accept that the burning bush truly signifies God's presence. And furthermore, God's presence is so powerful that he'd better not try to look at God. And third, when God tells Moses about the merciful and gracious act God is about to perform for the Hebrews enslaved in Egypt, all Moses can do is ask self-consumed questions about why God is picking on him for the job.

• Can we really blame Moses for his response to God's call? How might you have responded?

• What places come to your mind when you think of the term *Holy Ground*? Why do these places seem holy to you?

4. Prayer

Merciful God, you surprise us in the awesome ways you come to us. Help us respond to you with the appropriate fearful wonder and awe and with hands and feet willing to do what you desire of us. Amen.

Let My People Go
Exodus 5–7

1 Scouting the Terrain

These two chapters focus on the leadership training of Moses and Aaron and on the formation of the Israelites into a people, as opposed to independent families. We no longer read stories of family drama, now it's all about community drama and the relationship between leaders and followers. Moses and Aaron continually learn how to follow God's commands and the Hebrew people continually struggle with trusting Moses' and Aaron's leadership. The Hebrews respond to Moses and Aaron like fair weather friends. Their trust in God runs as deep as their circumstances suggest. When things start looking bad, everyone begins to doubt that God can really pull through and help them. Even Moses turns to question God and learns that it can be very hard being a leader. But God speaks and acts when the Israelites think life can't get any worse for them. When even the supposedly faithful leader, Moses, begins to doubt God's presence, God reminds Moses and the Israelites about the nature of this God. God reaffirms to Moses why everything is happening, to keep the covenant promises. There is a purpose here: the Israelites will be freed from Egyptian slavery and claimed by God.

Trailblazers

- God
- Moses
- Aaron
- Pharaoh

- Do different circumstances in your life cause you to feel nearer to or distanced from God? How so?

- What can you do in the times when you begin to doubt God's presence?

2 NOW READ EXODUS 5–7.

Road Signs

- **Ancestral houses:** another way of naming the twelve Israelites tribes
- **Nile:** Egypt's impressive river, an Egyptian source of life and sustenance

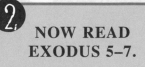

3 Switchback

Turning the water of the Nile into blood was a direct hit to the Egyptian's life source. The Nile was their main supply of water, and by contaminating it, God was showing one more way that the lives of the Egyptians were in God's hands. By getting his magicians to do the same thing, Pharaoh was simply showing his ruthless cruelty and pride. He was willing to put his own people's lives at stake just to battle with the Hebrews and their God. But at times, God's actions might even seem difficult for us to understand. In these chapters, God is willing to kill all the creatures of the Nile to prove God's point to the Egyptians.

• What are we to make of the fact that God creates and destroys according to God's purposes?

• When was the last time you struggled to accept something that God didn't cause but allowed to happen? What sort of explanations did you think of?

4 Prayer

Almighty and Creator God, we don't always understand your actions; and it seems that there are many sides of you that we still don't know. Help us to trust you with the things of this world we fail to understand. And please keep us from hardening our hearts to your work in this world. Amen.

When you read that God will harden Pharaoh's heart, making it so that Pharaoh will not change his mind and release the Hebrew people, it seems hard to swallow. It seems that God is unleashing these horrifying plagues to convince Pharaoh, all the while controlling him so that he will not change his mind. This runs counter to the justice and mercy that we've come to know of God.

The problem may lie in the language translation. In English, we assign the action to God. The way we read it, God is actively controlling Pharaoh's mind. But some biblical scholars say that in the original language there is no action. Rather, it is the presence or the idea of God that gives Pharaoh his bad attitude. Pharaohs were considered by their people to be gods. So, the suggestion that another god (in this case, the God) could be more powerful than them would be met with incredible indignation. To concede to the other god's demands would be admitting weakness, which could result in losing the throne.

The Plagues
Exodus 8–10

1 Scouting the Terrain

A conflict begins between kings, the King of Creation and the created king of Egypt, and the results have eternal ramifications. God will set the Israelites free but will also prove that God is Lord of all creation at all times. The nine other plagues point to the strife between humanity and God. We continue to witness God using creation to battle creation! Frogs, gnats, flies, locusts, even darkness, and more are used to oppress both humans and animals. There are two significant additions to this conflict between God and Pharaoh. First, God distinguishes between the Israelites who live in Goshen, the land where Joseph's family settled centuries ago, and the Egyptians. Second, this time God has instructed Pharaoh to let the Israelites go so they can worship God. Even in this request, God is reminding Pharaoh that the Israelites owe allegiance to God before any created being. And God is also letting the Israelites know that worship is always at the center of relationship with God. As always, there are those non-Hebrews in the narrative, this time they are Pharaoh's magicians, who recognize the God of Abraham, Isaac, and Jacob and appropriately fear this God.

Road Signs

- **Kneading bowls:** These bowls were used for mixing the ingredients in bread making.
- **Kiln:** This is a type of oven.

Trailblazers

- **God**
- **Moses**
- **Aaron**
- **Pharaoh and his magicians**

- Think back over what you've read so far, from Genesis 1–Exodus 10. Is there something God has done in any of these chapters that you think affects your future?

Another interesting part of Exodus is that it highlights the role of women in developing God's purposes. Sometimes the women act in courageous faith, fully aware of God, and at other times God uses the women without their even knowing it.

Find examples of women, who even though they are afraid, act courageously for God and without excuses. Then go to *www.amazingbiblerace.com* and take the quiz.

2. NOW READ EXODUS 8–10.

3 Switchback

Sometimes when we finish doing something, it's over and done with. It's something in our past and we can forget about it. That is rarely the case with God's actions. When God does something the effects remain with us well into the future, often even affecting the way we think about our past. In these Exodus chapters God tells the Israelites that God expects them to remember everything God is doing. God wants them to make these events part of their family histories, so that even their grandchildren will know of God's amazing ways. God wants the Israelites to seal God's actions into their memory.

Pharaoh on the other hand, seems to have a pretty bad memory. He keeps going back on his word, even as God continues to destroy the Egypt's land and people. He seems almost like two different people in the blink of an eye. Even his officials plead with him to give Egypt a break. But Pharaoh's pride seems to blind him to everything and everyone else.

• In what ways did Moses and Aaron have to rely on one another in order to serve God? Can you think of a time when you and someone else needed one another to do something faithful?

• Even in God's plagues against Pharaoh and the Egyptians, God extends mercy toward them. Where in each of the plagues do you see signs of God's mercy?

4 Prayer

Unchanging God, who is the same yesterday, today and tomorrow, transform our memories that we might see the work of your hand more clearly and tell of your faithfulness and love to friends and family. Amen.

Passover
Exodus 11–12

 Scouting the Terrain

Trailblazers

- **God**
- **Moses**
- **Aaron**
- **Pharaoh and his officials**

The final plague is significant for both the Egyptians and the Israelites. Not only does it prove God's might to Egypt but it is also the beginning of the Israelites' learning to mark time by God's activity in their lives. No longer will their days, months, and years be marked by the unjust orders of slave drivers and the common practices of the surrounding culture. God will not only free them from a life of slavery, but God will also redefine their understanding of time. We already know that a lot of God's activity in Exodus teaches the Israelites about faithful remembrance, but now God teaches them about community and the significance of ritual acts. A ritual is something we repeat regularly that gives some structure and has meaning for our lives. Whether we know it or not, the rituals we perform say something about the kind of lives we lead. In these chapters the Israelites are on the brink of being formed anew, into a people whose religious rituals point to how God desires them to find meaning in their lives.

Remembering the Passover is a way for the Israelites to relive their experience of God's faithfulness, God's liberating them from slavery, and God's defeat of their enemies. And when the Israelites reenact this event, they will teach their children about the power and mercy of God and so raise their families to be faithful and obedient to this God who saves them and keeps promises.

- What rituals does your family have? What do these rituals say about the kind of life you lead?

- What rituals do you wish were a part of your life? To what would those rituals point?

- Does your family have any significant memories that have helped shape your family's identity?

3 Switchback

The narrative of the last plague is very dramatic. At the stroke of midnight, every house cries out because the firstborn child has been killed. You can't help wondering whether this scene is payback for when Pharaoh murdered all those Hebrew baby boys. However, it's hard to feel good about this chapter, thinking of those innocent children dying. It reminds us of the innocent victims of war: children who are killed because of battles adults are fighting.

This passage is a good example of the complexity of God and the deep sin of humanity. Human sin has consequences, especially when human sin knowingly and freely before God. Pharaoh's sin of pride and cruelty had repercussions for him and for the innocent people around him. As we saw earlier, in Genesis, rarely does someone's sin affect that other individual. A community often shares the harmful effects of sin.

- Do you know of anybody who has suffered as a result of someone else's sin? What happened?

- What are some of the consequences of sin?

2 NOW READ EXODUS 11–12.

4 Prayer

Forgive us our sins, Lord, and remind us that our actions always affect other people. Amen.

Road Signs

- **Lintel:** This beam of wood or stone spans the uprights of a doorway or window and is used for support.
- **Passover:** When God passed over the Israelite homes during the night, all the firstborn children in Egypt died. The Passover is still remembered by Jews today.
- **Unblemished lamb:** The blood of a pure lamb was the required cover for Israelite households so that God would not kill them during the final plague.
- **Unleavened bread:** This flat, dense bread doesn't have the active yeast ingredient necessary to make it rise. The night the Israelites fled Egypt, they didn't have time to wait the hours it takes for bread to rise.
- **Hyssop** (HIS-uhp)**:** This flowering shrub has clusters of little flowers that were used like brushes to apply the blood on the doors.

Parting and Departing
Exodus 13–14

1 Scouting the Terrain

Yes, God took the firstborn of the Egyptians; but God also has requirements for those whom God liberates. The response of the Israelites should be worship, honor, ritual, and remembrance. They are to teach their children about who God is and what God has done, and they are to relive the events of liberation in ritual so that generations to come might also experience God's saving work. These things are especially necessary when the Israelites are living freely in foreign lands. It might be tempting for them to forget how much they needed God and how faithful God was to them.

Trailblazers

- **God**
- **Moses**
- **Aaron**
- **Pharaoh**

By demanding the firstborn of all living things, God shows that God also requests sacrifice from those who belong to God. God's claims on us should bear physical signs to remind us of God's mighty work in our lives but also to bear witness to others. Reminders of God's age-old promises border the instructions that God gives the Israelites. The God of Abraham, Isaac, and Jacob is not a God who forgets or goes back on promises. God's strength liberates and God's presence journeys with God's people, going before them and leading the way.

- What kind of physical signs in our own lives speak of God's mighty work?

- At what times in your life are you most likely to forget God's blessings?

- What does it mean for our faith that God is a promise keeper?

2 NOW READ EXODUS 13–14.

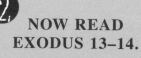

③ Switchback

God leads the Israelites into an impossible situation, seemingly trapping them between land and sea so that they will have to depend on God's strength and glory for freedom. But the Israelites fear for their lives and doubt both God and Moses. Throughout Exodus, the Israelites see-saw between saying that they believe and trust in God and then whining and complaining when things get tough. As for Moses, he's just getting started dealing with grumbling Israelites.

In the famous parting of the Red Sea, God used the chaos of water to both destroy life and save life. The Egyptians are conquered, and the Israelites walk on dry land in the parted water. God uses Moses to defeat the Egyptians. God may not need Moses' help, but God has chosen to accomplish God's purposes through humans.

- How would you describe the relationship between God and Moses?

- How do they rely on each other in the narrative?

④ Prayer

Thank you, God, for all of the times you have delivered me from danger and I haven't even known it. Teach me new ways to bear witness to your work in my life. Amen.

Road Signs

- **Month of Abib:** This is the name of the month when the Exodus occurred.
- **Consecrate:** This means to set apart as an offering to God for God's special purpose.
- **Philistines** (fi-LIS-teenz)**:** They were a brutish, warring people considered one of the Israelites' chief enemies. Modern-day Palestine gets its name from Philistine.
- **Succoth** (SUHK-uhth)**:** This was the first place the Israelites stopped to rest after making it out of Egypt. The name is Hebrew for "temporary dwelling."
- **Etham** (EE-thuhm)**, Pi-hahiroth** (PIGH huh-HIGH-roth)**, Baal-Zephon** (BAY-uhl-ZEE-fon)**,** and **Migdol** (MIG-dol)**:** These were Israelite rest stops along the way.

Water Break

You made it through Egypt with the Israelites! Weren't there times you wished that you could just knock some sense into Pharaoh or encourage the Israelites to hold on and have faith? Sometimes we can be as prideful as Pharaoh or as fearful as the Israelites. But thankfully, God is merciful even to the prideful and the fearful.

Singers and Whiners
Exodus 15–16

1 Scouting the Terrain

The defeat of the Egyptians leads the Israelites to praise and proclaim God's strength and victory. Moses and Miriam sing songs that celebrate God as a mighty warrior who fights on behalf of the oppressed. The poetic song lyrics reflect God's command of Creation and God's awesome reputation throughout the world. Even non-Egyptians tremble at the reputation of this God. God's victory not only frees the Israelites from slavery but also serves to witness God's majesty in the world. Victory is about proclaiming God's identity as the one who liberates captives. Another equally important fact being celebrated is that the cruel and tyrannical leaders of the world do not have the final word. When people are being oppressed under unjust governments, there is reason to hope in God's deliverance from suffering and another chance at new life lived in freedom and community. And the first response of those who are newly freed is to worship this God of liberation.

Trailblazers

• **Moses**
• **Miriam**
  (Moses' sister)

• Can you think of any countries today whose people could use such hope in God? What is going on in the country you selected?

• What do you think about the fact that God is being portrayed as a warrior in this Exodus story?

Road Signs

• **Marah** (maw-RAW): The Hebrew word for "bitter," this is the place where the Israelites complained of no suitable water to drink.
• **Elim** (EE-lim): This is the next place the Israelites stopped after Marah.
• **Omer** (OH-muhr): This ancient standard of measurement equals about two quarts of dry goods.
• **Manna** (MAN-uh): This flaky, white, sweet substance that God rained down from heaven fed the Israelites every morning for the forty years of wilderness wandering. Manna presents God's daily provision, giving enough to meet everyone's needs.

2 NOW READ EXODUS 15–16.

48

③ Switchback

Just three days after singing songs of praise, the Israelites begin to complain to Moses. Instead of being led straight to the Promised Land, they find themselves in the wilderness without food or water. Without the security of knowing when they will eat and drink, the Israelites would rather be back as slaves in Egypt. They need to trust God for their basic needs. God begins to lay down some standards for how this newly freed people will work to become a faithful community in covenantal relationship with God. Their safety and care are dependent on their obedience to God. They will have to learn to listen to God and to trust God's provision.

It would be so easy to shake our heads at those stubborn Israelites, who can't seem to get it right. But in a lot of ways, we are like the Israelites, whooping it up when things are going well in our lives and complaining when things don't go as we'd like. Yes, the Israelites should be better at trusting God; but imagine being in their shoes. They were slaves for years under Pharaoh, wondering whether God even remembered them. Trust takes time to build.

• God provides the people with double amounts of food on the day before the Sabbath. What might this teach us when we say we are too busy to take time to worship God?

• Has there ever been a time when you've had trouble trusting God? What happened?

④ Prayer

Thank you, God, for all the times you have delivered me from danger and I hadn't even known it. I pray to celebrate you more in my life and to offer joyful thanksgiving for the blessings you give me. Amen.

What happens to the Israelites once they've been freed from slavery? This week we'll read about their wanderings in the wilderness. Although they grumble and complain, God's people find that God is faithful to provide for them. In chapters 15 through 18, find five ways that God provides for the Israelites. Then go to *www.amazingbiblerace.com* **to take a quiz.**

Not Deserted in the Desert
Exodus 17–19

1 Scouting the Terrain

The Israelites encounter their first battle in the wilderness. We meet for the first time Joshua, a warrior selected by Moses to lead the people through a holy war against the Amalekites. This battle is the beginning of many the Israelites will fight to reach the land God has promised them. And God remains on their side in battle. The circumstances of this battle reveal the communal effort needed for the Israelites to journey successfully through the wilderness. Moses, Aaron, Hur, and Joshua all play significant but different roles in the battle. Of course, God is ultimately behind the victory.

Then Jethro visits Moses, and we learn two main things from his visit. First, Jethro's response to Moses' retelling of the Israelite/Egyptian adventures shows us the power our stories of God have to transform our listeners. Never underestimate what God might do when you simply tell others what God has been doing in your life. Jethro praises God and acknowledges God's superiority. Second, Jethro's wise advice to Moses about being a counselor and judge to the Israelites shows us that even good leaders can always learn something from those with more experience and wisdom, and faithful leaders know when to listen to advice. Moses' leadership skills are sharpened during the visit with his father-in-law.

Trailblazers

- **God**
- **Moses**
- **Aaron**
- **Joshua**
- **Jethro** (Moses' father-in-law)
- **Hur**
- **Amalek and the Amalekites**

• When have you been given some good advice? Who gave it to you? What was the advice?

• Whom do you know that you consider to be a good leader? What makes this person a good leader? What qualities does he or she possess?

2 NOW READ EXODUS 17–19.

Road Signs

- **Rephidim** (REF-i-dim)**:** This was a place in between the wilderness of Sin and the wilderness of Sinai. This is where God provided water from a rock to quench the thirst of the complaining Israelites.
- **Inquire of God:** Ancient people believed that they could find out God's purposes by consulting specific persons who could communicate with God.
- **"Do not go near a woman":** God wanted the Israelite men to maintain sexual purity for a few days before approaching God.

3 Switchback

In the wilderness of Sinai, God tells Moses to gather the people so that God can affirm Moses' leadership role in front of the Israelites. However, a meeting with God is not carried out without the proper preparations and knowledge of human boundaries. The Israelites have to spend two whole days making themselves clean enough to approach God's presence. And even then, there are still limits to how near they can come to the mountain where God will be. Just like when God appeared in the burning bush, God's presence on the mountain transforms the mountain and its surroundings into holy ground.

Moses has to be the mediator between God and the people because the holiness of God is too overwhelming for humans to survive. God even threatens to destroy anyone who tries to approach the limits. All of the drama of God's appearance, such as the thunder and smoke and trumpet sounds, helps indicate what an awesome and somewhat frightening experience this meeting was for the Israelites. God calls the Israelites to be a holy people set apart, "a priestly kingdom." Their community should be centered on their identity as the people God led out of Egypt and with whom God entered a holy covenant.

4 Prayer

Holy God, your word reminds us to prepare ourselves to come into your presence. You no longer require ritual cleaning from your children; but please teach us how we should prepare our hearts, minds, and bodies to hear you and to commune with you. Amen.

- Of what communities are you a part? What binds each of these communities together? What is the shared identity of each of the communities?

- When have you experienced the awesome presence of God?

The Ten Commandments
Exodus 20–21

1 Scouting the Terrain

The Ten Commandments are also called the *Decalogue*. They can be divided into two parts: laws concerning people's relationship to God and laws concerning people's relationships to their neighbors. The first thing God does in the giving of the Law is remind the people who God is, what God has done for them, and what God requires in return for liberation. Freedom doesn't come without a divine price tag on it. When God frees people, God expects them to turn and give their lives back to God. It is a freedom to become bound to God. That's not the kind of freedom we usually think about, is it?

Some of these commandments might seem like random rules, but God had a reason for all of them. The main goal was for the Israelites to learn that, as followers of this particular God, they were to become a people distinguishable from all other people around them. The specifics of these commandments went against the common worship practices of neighboring people. It was common for people to worship a variety of gods for different needs. Statues of these gods were often constructed out of natural materials and metals, such as wood, gold, and silver, and treated as though they actually had divine powers. People also believed that you could use a god's name to get what you wanted, because knowing someone's name somehow gave you an added advantage over them. The first three commandments addressed these non-Israelite practices.

Road Signs

- **Alien residents:** These were non-Israelites who lived among the Israelites.
- **Hewn stones:** These stones were chiseled and shaped into ornamental altars.
- **Awl:** This is a tool with a pointed tip used to mark or pierce things.

Trailblazers

- **God**
- **Moses**
- **The Israelites**

- How do you define the word *neighbor*? Whom do you consider your neighbor?

- Do we worship false gods today? In other words, what things are we often more passionate about than God?

2 NOW READ EXODUS 20–21.

3 Switchback

God's presence is too much for the Israelites to bear, so they beg Moses to be the go-between guy from now on. And interestingly enough, this time is the last the Israelite people have such an intimate encounter with God, without a mediator. Perhaps imagining such fear of God is difficult; because many of us are used to thinking of God in the form of Jesus Christ, pictured with gentle eyes and surrounded by smiling children. Jesus is God, and God is love; but the divine awesomeness of God cannot be contained in pictures of a laughing man with smiling children. The Exodus text describes God's presence in dense clouds, in deep darkness, and in loud thunder. Even though this description is not necessarily a comforting one of God, we can give thanks that we serve this God, who is beyond our understanding and our control and who is capable of giving us new life and sustaining us in all things.

• Which commandments do you think might have been the most difficult for the Israelites to keep? Which commandments do you think people in our world struggle with most?

• What, do you think, does God mean by saying, "I am a jealous God"?

Racing Tip

Lex Talionis (LEX tal-EE-OH-nis)**:** This was the law that put limits on how much someone could be punished for a crime. "An eye for an eye, a tooth for a tooth" was a law that focused on fair punishment rather than on getting revenge.

4 Prayer

Merciful Lord, your commandments teach us how to behave as children saved by your love. Help us live so that other people can witness how your love changes people. Amen.

fast forward Spend some time with your team looking through popular magazines, watching commercials and entertainment television. Create a piece of art, write and perform a skit, or write a song that conveys the modern-day idols to which we give more devotion than we do to God. Take a photo or video and upload it for points.

Laws and Commandments
Exodus 22–23

① Scouting the Terrain

God did not free the Israelites so that they could mistreat other people. God freed them so that they could be an example of what a just society looks like by God's standards. The Israelites were being formed into people who would take care of those in need and who would become family to those without families. Compassion for others would come before self-interests, and the poor would be treated fairly. God reminds the Israelites that just as God heard their cries in Egypt, so too will God hear the cries of those who are treated unjustly by the Israelites. God's sense of justice even includes treating one's enemies fairly and not ignoring opportunities to do the right thing, even if it will benefit someone you dislike or who dislikes you. All of these laws continue to show the Israelites that obedience to God affects all aspects of daily living: economic, social, sexual, and personal. The many laws regarding the treatment of animals are because the people were part of an agricultural community. Animals were a vital part of their livelihood, so how they cared for one another's animals had a significant effect on the community. Plus, healthy communal living, the way God intends, means that people need to treat one another with respect and care and to realize their dependence on one another.

Trailblazers
- **God**
- **The Israelites**

• Why are rules and laws necessary?

• What are some unwritten rules that everybody generally adheres to because doing so improves the quality of life for everybody?

• What is a rule that you have to live by that you think is unnecessary? Why, do you think, does the rule exist?

② NOW READ EXODUS 22–23.

3 Switchback

The laws of Chapter 23 further acknowledge that God is also a God of renewal, a God who cares for non-human creation, a God who cares for the poor and the weak, and a God who values life and justice more than money and power. Even animals and the earth deserve rest. The laws acknowledge that those who are poor and without farming land need to gather food. God made all of creation and honors it by creating a calendar that teaches the Israelites how to be good stewards of the earth, recognizing God's sovereignty and always remembering to provide for those in need, human and animals. Again, this chapter is an example of how the Israelites learn new ways to mark time.

- In our culture, we tend to live as though being busy all the time gives us a sense of purpose. But God says that taking time to be still and to rest is not only a very purposeful way of living but also part of spiritual worship and obedience. What do you think about that idea? What in these laws can we learn about living as a community of God's people?

- Think about your community at school. Is there anything in these laws that could speak to how relationships are sustained in your school community?

- How is the calendar of your culture marked? What are the significant points of the year, and what do these times represent?

Road Signs

- **Bride price:** This is the amount of money given a father for the use of his daughter. Women were considered property of the men of their households.
- **Festival of Unleavened Bread:** This celebration recognizes the Passover during the escape from Egypt.
- **Festival of the Harvest:** This celebration takes place in June, when wheat is harvested.
- **Festival of Ingathering:** This autumn celebration takes place when the crops are ready to be harvested. God desires the first fruits, the best of what the people require for living.
- **Amorites, Hittites, Perizzites, Canaanites, Hivites, Jebusites:** These are the people that God drove out of the land so that the Israelites could have it.

4 Prayer

Lord of all creation, teach us to be better stewards of the earth and to find faithful ways of slowing down our busy lives. Amen.

We're in a Committed Relationship
Exodus 24–25

1 Scouting the Terrain

Trailblazers

- **God**
- **Aaron**
- **Nadab and Abihu** (sons of Aaron)

There are two key things going on in Chapter 24: God stops giving laws for a short time for some self-revelation, and Moses leads the Israelites through a covenant ceremony where they vow to be obedient to God and to God's words. God and Israel have pledged themselves to each other.

Let's focus on God's self-revelation. The name for God's act of revealing God's self is "theophany." We can learn a lot from the details surrounding God's self-disclosure. Here is a list of those details:

1. Moses **is invited** to come before God.
2. Moses **makes an altar** before the mountain where God dwells.
3. Moses goes up to **meet with God**.
4. Moses and the priests and elders **saw God** and ate and drank before God.
5. Moses **waited for God.**
6. Moses **entered the cloud of God's presence.**
7. As viewed by the people from the bottom of the mountain, **God appeared as "devouring fire."**
8. Moses **was gone** for 40 days and nights.

- What do the bold face words suggest about God and about Moses' experience?

- If God invited you into God's presence, what steps would you take to prepare for the meeting?

- Have you ever been invited into God's presence? Think hard.

WEEK
5
◇
DAY
5

2 NOW READ EXODUS 24–25.

3 Switchback

After God and Israel commit to each other, God takes the relationship one step further and amazingly offers to come live with the Israelites. That's how much God loves God's people. But it is still a relationship of Creator and the created. God is still holy and requires certain standards. The instructions for the Tabernacle tell us a lot about how God desires to be worshiped. The first is that God wants people to *want* to worship God and to desire God's presence. By asking Moses to collect an offering of materials, God is clearly indicating that people will not be forced to worship. But for those who do, there are God-ordained ways to do so. All of the furnishings of the Tabernacle emphasize God's holiness and life-giving capabilities and the need for humans to humbly acknowledge and faithfully obey this God.

- Do you think that it would be better if God forced everybody to worship and adhere to God's will?

4 Prayer

Almighty God, thank you for your desire to dwell among us and to be our God. Forgive us when we fail to see you in all of the ways you reveal yourself in our lives. Give us new eyes to see you and deeper hearts in which to make you a home. Amen.

Road Signs

- **Ark:** This wooden chest served as God's throne and as the place where the commandments and laws were kept.
- **Acacia** (uh-KAY-shuh)**:** This is a type of tree.
- **Mercy seat:** This is the cover on top of the ark that is the place where God covers up the sins of the people and meets with the priests to give God's commandments.
- **Tabernacle:** This is the movable temple where God chooses to "live" in the presence of the Israelites while they are without a permanent home.
- **Bread of the Presence:** This sacramental offering of bread is either eaten by the community or offered up to God in the sanctuary. It symbolizes God's constant provision.

Water Break

Nice going! You're more than halfway through the second book of the Bible. This week, you have read through a very challenging section. The story the Hebrews' exodus from Egypt, with all of the plagues, the drama in the desert, and the receiving of the Ten Commandments, is a lot to contemplate and take in. But you made it. Congratulations!

The Tabernacle
Exodus 26–28

① Scouting the Terrain

The instructions for building the Tabernacle are both detailed and ornate. God knows exactly what the place should look like. It's interesting to imagine God's decorative sense. We rarely consider God's appreciation of beauty; but from what we can read about the details of the Tabernacle, it is obvious that God finds pleasure in how things look. The priestly garments are decorated with jewels and ornate hem patterns. The furnishings are made of fancy metals and sweet smelling beautiful wood with intricate carvings. The curtains are colorful and made of fine linens. God was creating a place to be with the Israelites and still maintain a holy distance, and clearly God desires the very best.

Trailblazers
- **God**
- **Moses**

The Tabernacle was where the Israelites went to encounter God, and the place where the priests would make up for the sins of the people. Aaron was to be made the high priest, who got to enter into the most holy place to represent the people. Being in God's presence was such a holy and sacred event that one had the possibility of dying. So the high priest had to have a rope and a bell tied to him when he entered the holy place so that in case he died, the people could drag out his body.

- God ordered the building of the Tabernacle so that God's presence would be right there among the Israelites. What does it mean to us that God lives with us and is accessible to us?

- How would things be different if this closeness were not the case?

② NOW READ EXODUS 26–28.

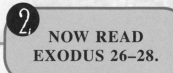

3 Switchback

The priests are elected to serve God before serving anyone else, even before the community of Israel itself. These holy men will be distinguished by their clothes and by the rituals they perform. And they will have emblems hanging from their foreheads, acknowledging that they belong to God. People will recognize them as servants of God and will bear witness to God's holiness. As Christians, we believe that we are all servants of God, all called to be holy.

• Some Christians wear priestly vestments that mark them as God's servants; but for those of us who are not pastors, priests, monks, or nuns, what about our presence makes us recognizable as God's servants? How do we bear witness to God's holiness?

• What does such a variety of building materials and detailed instructions suggest to you about God?

• What do you think of the idea that someone could die in God's presence? Does that make sense to you? Why, or why not?

4 Prayer

Dear God, because you appreciate beauty, help us recognize beauty when we see it and not be afraid to embrace beautiful craftsmanship in our own lives. Amen.

Road Signs

• **Urim and Thummin** (YOOR-im) (THUM-im): These were dice used to determine God's will.

• **Tent of meeting:** This was different from the Tabernacle. It was a tent, away from the camp, where God met with Moses.

• **Ephod:** The robe-like part of the priests' wardrobe needed to enter God's presence.

• **Signet:** This device was used to stamp ownership or identification onto something. In Old Testament times, it was a stone with writing cut into the surface and was dipped into clay or wax to make the mark.

The Way to Worship
Exodus 29–31

1 Scouting the Terrain

Priests are set apart for participating in the sacrificial offerings to God. Aaron and his descendants will be the priests of the people. The Israelite life with God will be marked by holiness, sacrifice, daily worship, and reverence. Coming before God requires specific rituals that highlight God's divine holiness and the inadequacy of humanity. The appointed priests must be cleaned, anointed, and appropriately clothed. The instruments and furnishings of the Tabernacle must also be prepared for God's divine habitation. To welcome or receive God into our midst requires holy preparation and recognition of the differences between God and humanity.

Trailblazers

- **God**
- **Moses**
- **Aaron and sons**

- In what ways do we prepare ourselves to go before God?

- Do you think that it was a blessing or a burden on the priests to have been chosen by God? Why?

Road Signs

- **Sin offering:** This animal sacrifice was used to seek forgiveness of sins.
- **Holy diadem:** This is an object hanging on the priests' turban that falls in front of their foreheads. The words *Holy to the Lord* are written on it.
- **Hin:** This liquid measurement is slightly less than a gallon.
- **Frankincense:** This sweet tree gum was used to make the only incense allowed on the altar table.
- **Burnt offering:** This was a daily offering of worship.
- **Stacte** (STAK-tee): This tree sap was used to make incense.
- **Myrrh:** This sweet-smelling tree gum was considered very valuable. It was used for many things: to make incense, as perfume, and to embalm the dead.
- **Elevation offering:** This is the act of taking something from the altar and bearing it up to God with one's hands, symbolizing that one lifts all things up to God.
- **Onycha** (ON-i-kuh): This is an incense ingredient from a shellfish.
- **Galbanum** (GAL-buh-nuhm): This plant sap was used for incense.

2. NOW READ
EXODUS 29–31.

Exodus

3 Switchback

Chapter 31 reminds us that God gifts people with a variety of skills in order to honor and serve God. Usually, when we think of serving God or being in ministry, we imagine that we have to be ordained clergy. But the tailors and craftspeople are also servants of God. They are artists with skills given by God, and they use those skills to serve God. We tend to forget that God gives us all types of gifts and that all of our skills and talents can be used to serve God. Being an artist, a poet, a writer, a carpenter, an architect, a jeweler, or a farmer can all be means of serving God. It takes time and practice to figure out what skills God has given you and how to use those skills to serve God.

Along with using our gifts to serve God, we also need to remember to rest from work, as God commands us. The other important piece of Chapter 31 is God's instructions on keeping the Sabbath. Right after God informs Moses of the gifts and skills to be used for work, God instructs Moses to appoint a holy day of rest, a non-optional time where people must cease from their work and acknowledge God's own labor and rest during Creation. If God can accomplish in six days all that is needed, then we can as well. We can trust that God's marking of time is sufficient for us and remembering that the world is sustained by God's work, not ours.

• What are some skills with which you think God has gifted you?

• Why is it so hard in our culture to keep the Sabbath as a holy day of rest?

4 Prayer

Generous God, thank you for the skills and talents you give us. Help me to continually discover the ways in which you have gifted me and to use my gifts to serve you. Amen.

Make a list of all of the different colors, all of the different metals, and all of the different types of materials used in making the Tabernacle. Take a quiz at *amazingbiblerace.com* to see how much you've learned about the tabernacle materials and to get additional instructions for a special second part to this weekly challenge.

Unholy Cow!
Exodus 32–33

WEEK
6
◇
DAY
3

1 Scouting the Terrain

We have just read God's instructions for holiness and how God desires to be the God of the Israelites, who liberates them and journeys with them. Moses is about to go down and tell Aaron all that God has planned for him as the high priest to serve as representative for the people. But at the same time, at the bottom of the mountain, Aaron and the Israelites are determining their own standards for holiness and worship. We read on to witness their lack of faith and their willingness to abandon the God of Abraham, Isaac, and Jacob—the God who freed them from slavery to the Egyptians. With the gold God has just asked Moses to collect for the building of the Tabernacle, the unfaithful Israelites build a golden calf, a false god that neither hears nor speaks, a powerless god created by humans. And the very rituals that God desires them to conduct before God they perform before the lifeless calf statue. While God is graciously devising a means by which the people can remain in relationship with God, the people are busy being impatient with God's timing and not trusting God's promises.

Trailblazers

• God
• Moses
• Aaron
• Joshua

• God must have been very disappointed in the Israelites. When was a time that you were disappointed? What caused this disappointment? How did you move on?

• Despite God's continuous provision and guidance, the Israelites quickly lost faith after Moses had left them for a few weeks. Even though you know that you have been blessed in many ways, what things can sometimes call your faith in God into question?

2 NOW READ EXODUS 32–33.

3 Switchback

Moses had a friendship with God such that he and God would meet regularly to talk. And when they talked, nothing was off limits. Moses felt free to ask God to reconsider decisions, to prove God's affection toward him, to journey with the Israelites, and even to ask God to reveal all of God's holiness to him. Theologians (people who study the Bible and the ideas about God) have long spoken about the hidden nature and simultaneous revelation of God. The point is that God, being full of grace, wants us to experience and be in relationship with God. However, some aspects of God remain a mystery. God is still holy and beyond what we can ever fully understand. Moses' experience with God is a good example of this.

Exodus

- How does Moses get God to reconsider destroying the unfaithful Israelites? Why, do you think, do God and Moses have such a special relationship?

- What can we learn about God from God's response to the golden calf?

- Why, do you think, does the Bible emphasize that the tablets of the covenant were written by the finger of God?

- In what ways have you experienced God's hidden nature and revelation?

Road Signs

- **Golden calf:** Creating idols to worship was common pagan practice.
- **Mount Sinai:** This is the mountain where God and Israel made their covenant, where God spoke to Moses and revealed God's self. In the Bible, mountains are often associated with religious experiences.

4 Prayer

Merciful God, forgive us for the idols we make in our lives. Help us wait for your perfect timing in all things, to trust the promises you make us through your Word, and to worship you alone. Amen.

Ten Commandments, Take Two
Exodus 34–36

1 Scouting the Terrain

Before offering to *rewrite* the Ten Commandments for the stubborn and unfaithful Israelites, God points out that this second chance is an act of memory and grace, love and faithfulness; but God also emphasizes that there are consequences when people sin. This is a hard thing to understand, how God both forgives sin and punishes sin.

Trailblazers

• **God**
• **Moses**
• **Belzalel and Oholiab**
(craftsmen who will work on the Tabernacle)

There is also a new name for God: Jealous. The Israelites are called to worship and serve God alone. God knows how easy it is for us humans to be influenced by aspects of our surrounding culture that promise happiness and success without God's standards, and by peer pressure to do whatever everyone else is doing. Some people in history have used these chapters to suggest that God doesn't like different races of people to mix. Obviously that's wrong for many reasons: one being that God created and loves all people. What God seems to be objecting to in these passages is when the Israelites mix with other people who cause them to turn away from God.

After Moses encounters God so intimately, he is forever changed. His face shines brilliantly and he has to wear a veil. There are so many ways to interpret this beautiful part of the chapter. Maybe God's awesomeness is so great that Moses is forever stamped with the glow of God.

• Maybe Moses' glow symbolizes his special relationship with God and his survival after being in God's presence. What do you think?

• Why do you think God agrees to rewrite the commandments?

2 NOW READ EXODUS 34–36.

3 Switchback

The response of Israel is recommitment to obedience. They begin gathering the necessary items to build the Tabernacle for God. Notice the recurring theme of stirred hearts and willing spirits. Those who donate materials and help build the Tabernacle are the people who are spiritually moved out of love for God and a desire to prove their willingness to be obedient this time. All communities are made up of those who abandon God and readily donate to create the golden calf and those who readily donate for God, those who are quick to disobey and those who are quick to obey. Making a space for God to dwell makes demands on people's emotions, spirits, finances, and physical abilities. These chapters also speak to how everyone's gifts and efforts are needed to sustain faith communities.

• What gifts do you think you could bring to sustaining a faith community?

4 Prayer

Generous God, grant us willing spirits and generous hearts to use our gifts to build and sustain communities that worship you. Amen.

Road Signs

• **Cast idols:** These are the statues of pagan gods.
• **Festival of Weeks:** This celebration, also called Pentecost, started after Passover and lasted 50 days. It marked the time between the barley harvest and the wheat harvest, when the first offerings from the field were brought before God.
• **Altars, pillars, and sacred poles of non-Israelites:** These are the symbolic elements of pagan worship.

Tabernacle Furnishings
Exodus 37–40

1 Scouting the Terrain

Now that all of the instructions have been given and covenants reaffirmed, the Israelites can act on their pledged obedience and begin to build the Tabernacle for God. The point of restating so much of the building instructions is to point out that Israel is indeed faithful to God's commandments this time. Notice that Moses is pretty much out of the picture once the building begins. It is time for the skilled and gifted workers to use their gifts to serve God. All of God's people have their own unique calling, and these chapters continue to affirm that a variety of gifts are necessary for creating a community of faith. These chapters also show how hard humans had to work to create a space for God to dwell among them. Being faithful and obedient and welcoming God is not only a spiritual practice; it involves the use of our created bodies.

- What are some ways in which you use your own created body to be faithful and obedient and to welcome God into your life?

- What would you say were some of Moses' gifts?

Road Signs

- **Talent:** This amount of money equaled 3600 shekels.
- **Shekel:** This weight was used to measure monetary commodities. Money could be in the form of animals, jewelry, metal, weapons, or even food, depending on the historical time period.

Trailblazers

- **Belzalel and Oholiab** (craftsmen who worked on the Tabernacle)
- **The Levites**
- **Ithamar** (oversaw the work on the Tabernacle)
- **Aaron**
- **Moses**

WEEK 6 ◇ DAY 5

2 NOW READ EXODUS 37–40.

3 Switchback

Once the Tabernacle is finished the Israelites await God's coming. But first Moses has the job of arranging and anointing all the furniture and sanctuary objects so that all the things made from human hands can be consecrated and made appropriately holy for God. Then Moses must make the priests holy through a ritual cleansing. Moses is able to do all these things because of the authority God gives him. Not just anyone can take human-made objects and make them holy enough for God to receive or to dwell in. These moments are significant in Israel's history: they continue to emphasize God's grace and love in offering God's self to humanity.

So when God finally appears, God's presence is still beyond human understanding. God comes in a pillar of cloud and fire, revealed but still hidden, available but still beyond human reach, present but still in constant motion. Yet this magnificent God is still the guide, the protector, and the promise-giver and promise-keeper of God's people.

• In what ways is the relationship between God and God's people different today than in Moses' time? In what ways is it similar?

• What, do you think, is the most important thing to be learned from what you've read in the book of Exodus?

4 Prayer

Ever present God, by your Holy Spirit you have promised to be with us always. Our lives are a dwelling place for you, and our bodies are our instruments of worship. Help us do our part of faithfully receiving you and serving you. Amen.

Water Break

Another book is finished; another journey has ended. You've had another glimpse at the God of all creation and the dramatic life of the Israelites, our faith ancestors. You did it! You can now tell the story of the ten crazy plagues, the escape from Egypt, the golden calf fiasco, and the giving of the Ten Commandments. You are really becoming a biblical scholar. Well done!

Making Offerings to God
Leviticus 1–3

1 Scouting the Terrain

The name *Leviticus* comes from the priests who were called and set apart by God. These priests came from the tribe of Levi, descendants of Levi, one of Jacob's twelve son, so they were called Levites. This book is commonly regarded as the how-to guide for Israelite priests, but the ways of worshiping God described in these pages were meant to teach all of the Israelites to honor God and to live holy lives. We might not understand all of the sacrificial and cleanliness laws that God required of the Israelites; but we can, at least, learn that God is a God of order and holiness and requires the same standards for God's people.

Trailblazers

• **God**
• **Moses**
• **Aaron**
• **Priests**

• Why, do you think, does God have requirements for people before they come before God?

2 NOW READ LEVITICUS 1–3.

Road Signs

• **Burnt offerings:** These gifts symbolized daily worship and praise of God.
• **Grain offerings:** These gifts symbolized praise and thanksgiving and were taken from the first batch of one's own food source.
• **Salt of the covenant**: All food offered up was to be seasoned with salt. Salt sealed covenants.

• **Offering of well-being:** This was considered a way of communing with God to show thanksgiving and praise. A meal was shared by the people before God.
• **Suet:** This is the fat that surrounds an animal's kidney and loins.
• **An offering without blemish:** God requires of the Israelites a pure offering, an animal without disease or injury.

3 Switchback

The offerings made before God signify that the Israelites recognize the holiness of God. By grace, God has made it so that God is approachable; but there is still a big difference between divinity and humanity. The fact that there are three different types of offerings—burnt, grain, and well-being— suggests that those who approach God must acknowledge that God expects daily worship and praise. And God, the giver and sustainer of life, desires the best we have to offer, since all gifts and blessings come from God. God invites reconciled sinners into fellowship.

Is reading about offerings to God an uphill challenge? Don't sweat it. We'll give you a leg up.

Check *amazingbiblerace.com* for a "boost" about what all this offering talk means. Then take a short quiz to show that you've cleared the hurdle.

The burnt offering was considered the most important of the three because it was a daily reminder of the call to worship God and repent from sin. When a person made a burnt offering, he had to lay his hand on the animal symbolizing both a confession for his sins and the act of transferring his sins to the animal sacrifice. Only a repentant sinner could come before God to offer worship. After the sacrifice that reconciled the sinner to God (sacrifice of atonement), the grain and well-being offerings could be given.

• What is it about the sacrificial requirements that suggests that God desires the very best we have to offer?

• Does the idea of passing human sin onto a sacrificial offering remind you of Christianity in any way? How?

4 Prayer

Dear God, help us keep our own daily rituals of worship, confession, repentance, and praise. Amen.

Sin and Guilt Offerings
Leviticus 4–7

1 Scouting the Terrain

The opening words of Chapter 4 highlight a new section of the laws. Issues concerning sin are at the center of the next couple of chapters. Sin and guilt offerings are not optional for the Israelites. In order to cover those sins, God requires rituals of confession, repentance, and reconciliation for all who sin against God. The sins described in these chapters reveal a lot about what it means to be in relationship with God and about what it means to be a community. When someone sins against a neighbor. The offense is still against God because God desires that people live in loving and just relationships with one another.

Trailblazers
• God
• Moses

There are sins committed by accident and sins the individual is well aware of committing. In either case, once a sin is recognized, the person who committed the sin has to seek God's forgiveness. The destructiveness of sin is so great that when the religious leaders sin, the whole community is affected and bears the guilt of the offense. And no one in the community is too special or holy to fall into sin. Even priests and government leaders do sinful things sometimes. All humans are prone to sin. God knows that, and the amazing sign of God's love and mercy is that God offers sinners a way to make amends and return to holy relationship with God.

• As Christians, we are no longer required to make animal sacrifices to God or to make sin and guilt offerings. But are we still called to make offerings to God? Explain your answer.

• Being that we don't make animal sacrifices anymore, how do we make up for our sins?

2 NOW READ LEVITICUS 4–7.

3 Switchback

The guilt offering was considered to be different from the sin offering. The guilt offering provided a means to repent for injustices committed against other people that require some sort of payback. For both the sin and the guilt offerings, the representative piece was the blood and the fat of the sacrifice. Blood and fat are considered the essence of life and so are required for the covering of sins. In pouring out blood and offering up the fat, the sinner is symbolically offering up his or her life to God as a way of repentance. The punishment for sinning against God is death, so the sacrificial animal had to bear the sins of the sinner and give up its life in the sinner's place. The parts of the animal considered unclean had to be taken away from the camp to be burned completely. God did not want any aspect of the sin, represented by the animal, to exist in any form in God's presence or in the presence of God's people.

• How does God ensure that even the poorer people in the community will be able to make amends for their sins?

• From verses such as 6:27, it seems that holiness was considered contagious by touch. What are some ways that we could think of holiness as contagious today?

4 Prayer

We thank you, Lord, for your deep love, enabling you to present yourself—through Jesus Christ—as the sacrificial offering for our sins. Help us learn the many ways we can still offer our lives up to you. Amen.

Road Signs

• **Offering of ordination:** The blood of the sacrifice was used to make peace between God and the man who was to be ordained as high priest.
• **Altar of fragrant incense:** Incense was considered holy and was used in sacred worship rites.
• **Elders:** These were the senior men of the Israelite community who held positions of leadership overseeing justice.
• **Holy things:** These are tithes and offerings to God.

Ordaining the Priests
Leviticus 8–10

1 Scouting the Terrain

The ordination of the priests was a significant communal event. The priests were the mediators to God. They were chosen by God and were called to a life of holiness beyond the standards expected of the rest of the community. So it was no surprise that the ordination ritual took at least seven days. Aaron and his sons were preparing for a lifetime of service to God; and like anyone else who approached God, they too had to make their sacrificial offerings. Everything that had anything to do with the event was consecrated and made holy with the anointing oil. Everything was carried out just as God had commanded Moses back on Mount Sinai. Moses continued to be completely obedient to God, always a witness and an example for all the Israelites.

Notice that there aren't any women priests being consecrated. The role of priests was restricted to men, not just in Israelite culture but in most surrounding cultures at the time. Women's roles were primarily restricted to childbearing, agriculture, and household services. Some biblical scholars have suggested that the only priestly roles available to women were probably related to sewing priestly vestments, handling Tabernacle furnishings, and cleaning the utensils and dishware used for worship.

Trailblazers

- **Moses**
- **Aaron**
- **Nadab and Abihu**
  (Aaron's sons)

- Do you think that women also would have made good priests? Why, or why not?

- Do you think that it was stressful to be a priest?

- Aaron was appointed to the position of high priest despite his role in forging the golden calf. Does this seem right to you? What can we learn about God from this?

② NOW READ LEVITICUS 8–10.

③ Switchback

Right after the newly consecrated priests had finished their first worship service, the seriousness of God's call is put to the test when Aaron's sons sin. If God hadn't punished Nadab and Abihu for their disobedience, people would not have taken the priesthood duties as seriously as God had commanded them. The priests had to be faithful to God; otherwise, the rest of the community would bear their guilt. Being a priest meant putting God first and the welfare of the community second. Nadab and Abihu were Aaron's sons, but Aaron was instructed not to mourn their death. As a priest in the midst of being consecrated to God, he was not permitted to focus on anything else, even the death of his sons.

• What do you think about Nadab and Abihu's dying for their sacrilegious actions?

• What, would you say, is sacred today? Have you ever observed anybody's handling a sacred object or conducting a sacred ritual? If so, what struck you about that?

④ Prayer

Merciful God, sometimes when you direct our steps, we turn around and disobey you. We ask for your forgiveness and pray that you would help us learn how to commit ourselves to your ways. Amen.

Road Signs

• **Ordination:** This is the religious ceremony in which someone publicly goes through the rites to become a priest.
• **High priest:** This is the one priest chosen by God to be the main representative of the people. Only the high priest could perform certain holy services and enter into the holiest parts of the sanctuary.
• **Censer:** This is a container used to burn incense in.

Living for God Every Day
Leviticus 11–12

① Scouting the Terrain

Trailblazers
- **God**
- **Moses**
- **Aaron**

In the next five chapters, we move away from the offerings and rituals of sanctuary worship and, instead, focus on how God calls the Israelites to be set apart even in the normal "everydayness" of life. These chapters have to do with God's purity laws. God provides dietary regulations to the Israelites, separating the clean and acceptable food from the unclean and unacceptable food. In these cases, *clean* refers to being presentable for God. And God provides regulations for how people with diseases should be treated. The main point of all these rules and regulations is so that the Israelites learn that they are a people set apart by God. As a result, everything about their past life now has been altered. God gives them a new way of living and new daily practices, all constituting new standards of holiness. The only reason God gives for these seemingly random rules is that God is the LORD, who saved them from Egypt and that God saved them for a purpose. Now they live by God's rules; and God's primary requirement is that the people seek to be holy, just as God is holy.

- Just like holiness, uncleanliness is contagious. We know that the Scripture isn't talking about being physically dirty but, rather, being in an unacceptable state to come before God. As Christians, we are not required to keep these food laws. But do you think that we could ever be too unacceptable to come before God? Why, or why not?

② NOW READ LEVITICUS 11–12.

3 Switchback

It seems odd that women would have to go through purification periods after childbirth and that the times were longer if the baby was a girl. But even though we may not fully understand the reasons behind these laws, we do know that they do not represent any ideas of girl babies being less worthy than boy babies. Nor is childbirth considered an unclean act. Don't forget that the Creation story of Genesis says that God made man and woman in God's image and that God made them to go forth and multiply. Unfortunately, some people believe that God made men and women unequally; and they use certain Scripture passages, such as this Leviticus text, to support their claims. God made men and women with different gifts, but both sexes reflect God and should be treated with equal respect and value.

• Are there any signs in our culture today that suggest that men and women are not created equal? Explain.

• Are there any signs that suggest men and women are created equal? Explain.

4 Prayer

God of all people, we thank you for creating men and women, boys and girls in your image. Thank you for giving us different gifts so that we can complement one another. Help us see those gifts more clearly and recognize the blessings of having such differences. Amen.

This week we'll read the first fifteen chapters of Leviticus. This Old Testament book is a great challenge to us twenty-first century readers. It's full of descriptions of ceremonies, rituals, and rules. As you read, consider the following themes: 1) God is present with God's people; 2) Because God is holy, God's people must also be holy; 3) Since humans are sinful, they can't dwell with God. Contact between the sinner and divine holiness may result in death. Atonement for sin through sacrificial offering is necessary. Find passages in Leviticus that exemplify these themes named above. Then go to *www.amazingbiblerace.com* to take a quiz.

Good, Clean Living
Leviticus 13–15

1 Scouting the Terrain

These chapters are filled with laws about bodily cleanliness and uncleanliness. The priests have the responsibility of determining whether diseased persons are clean or unclean. And they have responsibility for performing the religious rites for cleaning those who are unclean. Disease can infect clothes and houses, as well as people. The disease under discussion is leprosy. There are many types of leprosy, and it's hard to know what exactly this biblical leprosy looked like. It is most likely that *leprosy* here refers to a number of different skin diseases on humans and a variety of molds and mildew on houses and clothes. It's important to note that the priests were not carrying out medical procedures. God's call to them was to cleanse the people for holy worship.

Rituals for cleansing included the sacrifice of a bird and the release of another bird dipped in the dead bird's blood. This ritual continues to emphasize the role of sacrificial and innocent blood in covering up the sins of the afflicted.

• These chapters describe physical ailments that would separate a person from the community. What else separates us from God's community?

• Do you know any songs from youth group or from church that reflect how Jesus' blood cleanses us from sin? Name some.

WEEK
7
◈
DAY
5

2 NOW READ LEVITICUS 13–15.

3 Switchback

Did you know that in ancient, biblical times, women had to be set apart for a week during their menstruation? Some scholars suggest that this time apart was required not because ancient, biblical people considered the menstrual cycle a bad thing; rather, women were separated from their spouses during this time so that their husbands couldn't have sex with them while the women felt physically and emotionally drained. Just as in the laws mentioned in previous chapters, these laws do not suggest that sex or human sex organs are considered bad. These laws were to teach the Israelite community about God's standards for cleanliness before they came to worship before God. And once they understood the difference between cleanliness and uncleanliness, God would instruct them on God's standards for holiness.

• What is the strangest-sounding law you have read about so far? Why, do you think, did it exist? Is there anything we can learn from it and apply to our lives today?

4 Prayer

Dear God, please remind us that you call us to worship you with our bodies as well as our hearts and minds. Amen.

Water Break

You made it through the first half of Leviticus. Did you know that most people who read the Bible take one look at Leviticus and pass it over? Now you can say that you have read half of it, and you can help others make some sense out of these laws and rituals that are often hard to understand. Well done! Only one more week of Leviticus to go.

The Holiness Code
Leviticus 16–18

1 Scouting the Terrain

The focus of chapters 17–26 is on the Holiness Code, the laws for the conduct of right living before God. But before we get to that, we need to focus on Chapter 16 and the ritual for the annual Day of Atonement, when the high priest sought to lay the sins of the people before God and seek forgiveness. A lot is going on in this ritual, but the two primary pieces are: God does not tolerate sin but requires life and blood for the cleansing of human sin; and God provides a way for individuals, and in essence, the whole community, to be cleansed from sin, without anyone having to die.

Trailblazers

• **God**
• **Moses**
• **Aaron**

Right after the death of Aaron's sons, God tells Aaron about the holy boundaries he needs to observe to prevent his own untimely death and to secure God's continued fellowship with the Israelite people. Once a year, the high priest, Aaron, must make atonement for the sins of the people. And Aaron must change his fancy high priest garments for the plain white clothes that ordinary priests wear. This shows that even he is humbled before God.

• In this system of animal sacrifices, the animals took the blame for the sins of the people. Have you ever been blamed for something someone else did? Have you ever been punished for it? What happened?

One of the most important verses in Leviticus is included in this week's reading of Chapter 17. Read through the chapter and see what jumps out at you as being meaningful.

Then read Genesis 9:4-6 and Hebrews 9:22. Go back and reread Leviticus 17 and see if you can pinpoint the verse that connects to the verses in Genesis and Hebrews. Go to *amazingbiblerace.com* to check your research by taking a short quiz.

2. NOW READ LEVITICUS 16–18.

3. Switchback

After instructing the people on seeking atonement, God addresses another crucial aspect of what it means to be in relationship with God: how to deal with the pressures of the larger cultures that don't follow God. The Israelites are being formed into a new people; they need to forget their past ways of living under the Egyptians and to be reminded not to fall under the ways of the Canaanites in the future. There is a long list of sexual no-noes that, along with addressing physical acts, also seem to be suggesting how people in different contexts should relate to one another. What we do with our bodies communicates more than we imagine. Then, at the end of the litany of taboos, God reveals an interesting point: The *land* suffers for the sinful actions of the people. What a thought! Not only are we reminded that the earth is God's creation, but we are also challenged to think about how even God's non-human creations suffer when we sin against God and against one another.

• Can you think of a modern-day example of how the land suffers by our human actions? Do you consider these actions a sin against God? Why, or why not?

4. Prayer

Thank you, God, for your Son Jesus Christ, the high priest, who makes atonement for our sins. Amen.

Road Signs

• **Cast lots:** This is the use of the Urim and Thummim dice to decide which goat is to be used for what purpose.
• **Goat-demons:** These idols of worship were popular in surrounding non-Israelite cultures.
• **Molech:** This was the god of the Ammonite people, who had a practice of making child sacrifices. God forbade the Israelites from such a monstrosity.

Laws Remixed
Leviticus 19–20

1 Scouting the Terrain

A lot of the laws stated in these two chapters are repetitions of laws we have already read. Remember how we noted at the beginning of this Bible race that a number of these texts were written by a couple of different writers? Well, some of those writers gathered information from more than one source; so sometimes the Scriptures repeat themselves.

Anyway, even with some repetition, we can still get some important information from these chapters. Notice how God makes sure that even the poor and the handicapped are taken care of and treated fairly? God is concerned about justice for all people, even the wealthy. Basically, God wants the Israelites to know that they have been called apart to be holy—because God chose them and because God is holy. Their holiness is simply a result of their being in covenant relationship with God. And being holy before God has consequences for how people live in their social communities, how they treat their parents, how they respect their elders, and how they learn to love and protect their neighbors. It even has consequences for how people conduct business and make a living for themselves. At the center of all these laws is relationship, relationship with God and with others.

Trailblazers
• **God**
• **Moses**
• **All of the people of Israel**

• In our American society today, how, do you think, do young people treat their elders? On what do you base your answer?

• Let's imagine something crazy for a minute. What if all of the store keepers at the mall were Christians who felt that their faith in God should make a difference in how they do business. What, do you think, are some things that might change?

2 NOW READ LEVITICUS 19–20.

3 Switchback

These chapters also reflect how much following God and being holy was the responsibility of all the people. Every member of society played a role in creating a faithful community where God would desire to dwell. It wasn't OK for a neighbor to choose not adhere to God's standards. The holy code of conduct was to help prevent people from profaning God's name and from putting the rest of their community in spiritual danger.

Reading through the laws in Leviticus is difficult for modern-day readers. We'll help you over this hurdle at *amazingbiblerace.com*.

It's OK to admit that we find some of the penalties for disobedience a little harsh. Imagine how many teenagers might be put to death for having cursed at or about their parents. The point is that these acts of disobedience are so offensive to God because they disregard God's order for Creation and for relationships that mirror aspects of God's divine image.

• Based on the scriptural passages, how does God make sure that people provide food for the poor amongst them?

• Do you think that God has any ideas about how we, today, should provide food for the poor amongst us? Explain.

4 Prayer

Dear God, please help us learn new ways we can give to the poor among us, the economically poor, the spiritually poor, and those who are poor in friendship. And help us to see the ways that we might be considered "the poor" by others. Amen.

Here is a perfect opportunity to assess how your group provides for the poor in your community. Get together with your team and discuss issues around poverty in your area. How can you live out the Scriptures by providing food or clothing for persons living in poverty? After you select your service opportunity, take a group photo or video of your team in action and upload it to *amazingbiblerace.com*. If you don't have a camera, write about it and post it as a blog on your profile page. Way to put the Word into action!

Proper Conduct Among the Priests
Leviticus 21–22

① Scouting the Terrain

In these two chapters, God instructs Moses on how the priests should conduct themselves. Those who have been set apart to serve God in the priestly role must live even holier lives than the average Israelite does. The first thing is that a priest must recognize that he has been set apart for God. God's demands overrule any other responsibility or inclination they may have as a regular Israelite living in community. So God begins by focusing on the priestly requirements for marriage and for mourning the dead, two of the most significant life stages, choosing a life long partner and dealing with the death of a loved one.

Priests could marry only virgins because virgins were considered the most pure state of womanhood. And because dead bodies were considered unclean, priests were only allowed to attend the funerals of their immediate family members. Remember, the priests and the high priests were the people allowed the closest into God's presence. So basically anything that threatened to make them unclean would bring uncleanliness into God's presence. So the priests had to live in such a way as to ensure that neither they themselves nor the dwelling place of God was made unclean.

Trailblazers
- **God**
- **Moses**
- **Aaron and the other priests**

• Do you think that there are certain types of Christians who should try to live holier lives than other Christians should?

• As Christians, we consider our bodies as one of the dwelling places of God because Jesus tells us that the Holy Spirit resides within us. How then can we treat our bodies as sanctuaries of God?

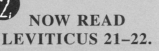

2. NOW READ LEVITICUS 21–22.

3 Switchback

Whew! What a long list of requirements for priesthood! It's a good thing God called the people to do it, because surely no one would have signed up for that. Seriously, all of the dos and don'ts listed in these chapters point to one thing: the holiness of God. Because the priest was the one who could get the closest to God, the priest had to remain pure so as not to defile God's holy presence.

When we get into the New Testament, we'll learn that our bodies are the new temples for God, that God isn't only in the holiest spot in the Temple building. Paul will tell us that our bodies are the temple for the Holy Spirit. So don't forget how important it is for the house of the Lord to remain pure and be a holy dwelling place for God.

• What sort of person comes to your mind when you imagine people in our times who have committed their entire lives to God? Describe how you think such a person looks, thinks, and acts. What personality traits do you imagine him or her having?

• Count how many times some variation of the phrase "I am the Lord your God" is repeated in these two chapters. Why, do you think, is this done?

Road Signs

• **Mourning customs:** Some of these customs included family members shaving their head and beard and mutilating their body.

• **Sacred donations:** This is the special food donated to the priests by the people.

• **Lay person:** This is a person who is not employed as a priest or other clergy.

Leviticus

4 Prayer

Dear God, your Word in the New Testament tells us that we didn't choose you but that you choose all of us. Thank you. Help us figure out the unique ways you desire each of us to serve you with our lives. Amen.

Jubilee
Leviticus 23–25

① Scouting the Terrain

Today's reading deals with many important aspects of Israelite holy living. Honoring the Sabbath and celebrating the works of God was a command, not an option. Sabbath rest is connected with worshiping God. In modern culture, when we think of Sunday as a rest day, we often associate that with the freedom to do whatever we please. We forget that God desires all creation to rest and to worship and acknowledge God. Festivals and fasts were observed throughout the year as a way for marking time but also as recognition of God's provision and our appropriate response of worship and self-denial.

Trailblazers

- God
- Moses
- the son of Shelomith

These chapters also address the severity of cursing God's name, the communal responsibility for carrying out punishment, and the hallowing of the name of God. When it comes to God's name, no one has special favor. We see more of God's sense of justice: People are punished according to the crime they commit, and everyone—whether Israelite or non-Israelite—follows the same law. Note that God's institution of the *Jubilee,* a time, every 50 years when all debts were cancelled and all slaves and indentured servants were released. Everyone got a new start. This was God's way of caring for the land and for those who must eke out a living through hard labor, indentured service, and heavy debt.

- Have you ever heard the word *Sabbath*? If so, what did you think it meant?

- Do you know anyone who practices the discipline of fasting? Why, do you think, do Christians still practice this discipline?

② NOW READ LEVITICUS 23–25.

3 Switchback

These chapters help us better understand how Jewish people mark the year. Continuing the tradition of the festivals and fasts remains a central and important part of Jewish life today. Jewish children are educated from an early age in the traditions and customs of their faith. By the age of 13, a Jewish child knows the story of the Israelites' escape from Egypt and all of the major commandments, laws, customs, and acts of remembrance that God required of the freed Israelites. The High Holy Days begin with Rosh Hashanah, the Jewish New Year, which falls in late September and lasts for 10 days. These are days of penitence. Yom Kippur falls on the tenth day, the Jewish Day of Atonement. On this day, Jewish persons fast and repent of their sins and the sins of humanity.

• What events do we remember by observing customs and traditions of the Christian faith? Why is it important to have these observances?

4 Prayer

Dear God, remind us that as Christians we also are a people with a story and that our story begins with the Israelites. Amen.

Road Signs

• **Feast of Unleavened Bread:** This holiday begins the day after Passover and lasts for seven days. The first and last day are days dedicated to God and no work is done.
• **Feast of First Fruits:** This holiday marks the beginning of the harvest time.
• **Festival of Weeks:** Also known as Pentecost, the Greek word for "fifty," this holiday marks the end of the harvest time.
• **Festival of Trumpets:** This holiday, celebrating the Israelite New Year, is marked with loud trumpet blowing.
• **Day of Atonement:** This is a day to repent of personal and communal sins.
• **Festival of Booths:** This holiday is a reminder of how the people lived during the Exodus years and a recognition of the end of fall harvest.

There's the Easy Way and the Hard Way
Leviticus 26–27

1 Scouting the Terrain

The prosperity of Israel and all creation connected to Israel is conditioned on Israel's obedience to God's laws and demands. The land, weather, and vegetation all are affected by Israel's relationship with God. Most important, God promises to walk among them and to be their God and they are to be known as God's people. If Israel is not faithful, the consequences are dire. The terrifying punishment that God describes is beyond imagination. But even beyond the possibility of such terror is the possibility of forgiveness and reconciliation.

Trailblazers

• God
• Moses

God's grace is present even in God's judgment of sin. If the fallen Israelites repent of their sin and disobedience and acknowledge God's terrifying actions as a result of their sin, then God will remember the promises to the patriarchs and restore the covenant. Ultimately, God desires to bless Creation, not to destroy it. God longs to be in a loving relationship with Creation, not in one of enmity. So have no doubt that God lays everything out on the table: God's expectations, what God's judgment of sin looks like, and how God deals with repentant hearts. The Israelites can surely never say, "But we didn't know!"

Road Signs

• **Uncircumcised heart:** This is a heart closed off to God.
• **"Passes under the shepherd's staff":** This term refers to a method of counting livestock.

• List a few ways you already know about concerning how God calls us to live so that you can't say, "But I didn't know," either.

• What do you think of this image of God who blesses so abundantly and also warns of such severe punishments?

2 NOW READ LEVITICUS 26–27.

3 Switchback

People often read Chapter 27 and wonder whether it is placed out of context, because it doesn't seem to flow naturally from Chapter 26. However, there's a different way to look at it. After reading Chapter 26, full of conditions and curses, it is a refreshing reminder to see that people make voluntary sacrifices to God out of love and personal desire. There were no requirements for people to make religious vows. But if they happened to do so, God had a way for them to go about it.

Remember that the key point of this whole book is that God desires for God's people to be holy because God is holy. The holy person's chief attitude before God is summed up in the first four commandments: Do not to worship any other gods, do not to make idols, do not to dishonor the name of God, and honor the Sabbath as a holy day. The standards for God's holiness represent God's knowledge of what it takes for us humans to be both faithful and truly walk on the path to abundant life.

• We already know that sin had a communal effect on the Israelites. If one person sinned, the whole community was affected. Do you think that human sin still has communal effects? How?

Water Break

You probably thought that you would never make it through Leviticus. Congratulations! We hope that you have come away with more than just a list of God's "dos and don'ts." You have received a little history lesson about some of modern-day Jewish customs. And believe it or not, having read Leviticus will help you get even more out of the rest of these first few books of the Bible. So press on now to the Book of Numbers, and continue your journey with the Israelites through the wilderness.

4 Prayer

Dear God, you demand certain standards of living if we are to follow you as true disciples. We pray to be obedient to your standards, not because we are fearful of your judgment but because we in love with you and with your ways. Amen.

Stand Still!
I'm Trying to Count
Numbers 1–4

1 Scouting the Terrain

The Book of Numbers opens with God speaking to Moses inside the Tent of Meeting as the Israelites are camped in the desert of Sinai. Moses is to take a census to determine the number of men who are old enough to serve in the army. God is preparing the Israelites to move into the Promised Land. Unfortunately, the Promised Land is already inhabited; and the Hebrews will have to fight their way in.

Trailblazers

- **God**
- **Moses**
- **Aaron**

Sometimes we tend to think that the Israelites were a small group of people traveling through the desert; but according to what we've read, there were 603,550 men over the age of 20. If we were to double that figure to include women and add in more for children and teenagers, we can assume that there were at least 1.5 million people in the Israelite community. How difficult it must have been, without printing presses or public address systems, for Moses and Aaron to adequately convey the Word of God to all of these people!

• Why, do you think, did God have Moses conduct a census?

• The first generation of Israelites wandered for forty years in the wilderness. What struggles might they have endured along the way? How do you imagine they dealt with these?

2 NOW READ NUMBERS 1–4.

3 Switchback

Once the census is taken, God tells Moses how the camp should be set up and the order that the people should march when they are on the move. The arrangement is based on the various levels of holiness and proximity to God. At the center of the camp is the Tabernacle, signifying God's presence in the midst of the people during their time in the wilderness. Then the people will set up camp farther away from the Tabernacle and grouped on all sides of it. After the Aaronic priests, the Levites will be closest to the Tabernacle because they are the people chosen by God to serve the priests. They are responsible for taking care of the Tabernacle and all its necessary equipment.

 hurdle Are all the names and numbers of Israelite tribes swimming around in your brain? It's a lot of information to process. Try this: make a diagram according to the details in Chapter 2. Mark north, south, east, and west on your paper and write down whose tribe was to go where. Jot down the number of persons associated with each group. When you're finished, check your work by completing our diagram online at *amazingbiblerace.com*.

Even though the Levites are all set aside for service to God, there still exist certain ranks and duties assigned to different groups of Levites. Aaron and his descendants are the chief priests and the other Levites are their assistants.

- Why, do you think, were such detailed instructions given about how to set up camp? What does this say about God?

- Is there something we can learn about the fact that God wanted the Tabernacle to be set up directly in the center of camp?

Road Signs

- **Census:** This is the term meaning the counting of a group of people.
- **Clan:** This is a group of families of the same tribe.
- **Kohathites** (KOH-huh-thights), **Gershonites** (GUHR-shuh-nights), **Merarites** (mi-RAH-rights): These were the Israelites selected to carry the Tabernacle and all of its equipment.

4 Prayer

Dear God, thank you for being a God of order and not of chaos. Help us to order our lives before you in ways that reflect your awesome holiness. Amen.

Standards of Purity
Numbers 5–8

1 Scouting the Terrain

A number of seemingly different circumstances are presented in chapters 5 and 6, but there is a central thread tying it all together. The main focus is on maintaining a healthy community in God's presence. It is important to remember that God is in the middle of all this, both literally (in the camp) and figuratively. All rituals, commands, and practices relate back to the Israelites' learning what is compatible with the holiness of God and what God cannot tolerate. Remember that conditions of purity and impurity have communal effects. One person's defilement puts the whole camp at risk. The continual question is, "How does one live within the boundaries of God's holiness?"

Trailblazers

• God
• Moses
• Priests
• Levities

These chapters simply begin with the conditions of impurity that put people the farthest from God, outside the camp. Those who are physically unhealthy are a risk to the purity of God's holiness, so they are put outside the camp. Then the Scripture moves on to the rituals of what to do concerning those within the camp who pose a threat to the cleanliness of others and to God's holiness. The scenarios deal with how to address social unrest, adultery, and contact with the dead by those people (Nazirites) who devoted their lives to God for a certain time period. Certain passages reveal that the concern here is not necessarily for the well-being of the people, their physical health, or emotional well-being. It is more about making sure that people do not sin against God by their actions of defilement.

• Why, do you think, could one Israelite's defilement put everyone around them in spiritual trouble?

2. NOW READ NUMBERS 5–8.

3 Switchback

Chapters 7 and 8 center on the sacrificial gift offerings of all of the tribes for the service of the Tabernacle and the cleansing of the Levites and ceremony for offering them up to God's service. Notice that the tribal offerings are given freely, without being commanded by God, and that all tribal offerings are equal before God. The whole Israelite community participates in the offering ceremony of the Levites. Commitment to God is never only a private affair. The Levites are different from the priests, and they serve two important functions. They serve the priests and help carry the Tabernacle and all its artifacts; and they camp close to the Tabernacle, where God resides, and serve as a physical barrier preventing the other Israelites from getting too close to God's presence.

• Have you ever considered that the Holiness of God can be dangerous? Is there anything for us to learn from the Israelites about giving in to God?

• The Levites cleansing ceremony is not a baptismal service but is reminiscent of one. What similarities to modern-day baptisms come to mind?

4 Prayer

Gracious God, help us give ourselves and our possessions freely to you, through tithing at church and by serving our less fortunate neighbors.

Numbers

Road Signs

• **"Water of bitterness that brings the curse":** This was a priestly mixture of water and dust, perhaps symbolizing life and death, of which the properties were believed to curse the guilty, adulterous woman or be ineffective on the falsely accused woman.

• **"(The woman) shall bear her iniquity":** This points out that the offense was against God and not against a jealous husband.

• **Vow of a Nazirite:** This religious vow to commit one's life to God was a set period of time. Nazirites were forbidden to cut their hair or drink wine while serving God.

• **The Aaronic Blessing:** This ancient blessing was used at the close of worship in the Jerusalem Temple.

• **Purification rites:** These rites included shaving the head and washing one's clothes.

Move 'Em Out
Numbers 9–12

1 Scouting the Terrain

After almost a year encamped at Sinai, the Israelites are commanded by God to start marching again. God is present with them through a cloud and fire. When the cloud stops, the Israelites stop and set up camp. The Israelites move when the cloud moves, and the Gershonites and the Merarites carry the Tabernacle in the middle of the procession. God's presence guides and protects the Israelites on the long journey filled with numerous stops. Yet even with God's presence and provision, conflict breaks out among the Israelites. First, they begin again to complain and to long for the old life of captivity in Egypt. Suddenly, God's provision is not worthy enough. They want the variety of food provided while they were slaves, instead of God's manna, described as sweet as cakes. Then Miriam and Aaron complain over Moses' qualifications for leadership. Even the ever-faithful and obedient Moses has his turn at complaining to God. Clearly, it has been a long trip for everyone; and you can almost hear children asking, "Are we there yet?"

Trailblazers

- **God**
- **Moses**
- **Miriam**
- **Aaron**

Understandably, God became annoyed with all of the complaining. God understands that Moses is beginning to feel the heavy burden of trying to lead such a stubborn people by himself. But as for the whining Israelites, who don't think that God has done enough for them, God gives them their fill of new food, quails enough to make them burst! And in the middle of their thankless gorging, God sends a plague to punish them for their greed.

• How is the journey of the Israelites like our own spiritual journeying?

• We usually think of God living up in heaven. How does God's presence with the Israelites conflict with the idea of a God far away in heaven?

• What does this suggest about how we can think about God today?

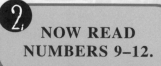

2 NOW READ NUMBERS 9–12.

3 Switchback

The dispute between Miriam and Aaron against Moses reveals a couple of things. First, Miriam is one of the few examples of female religious leaders in Scripture. Second, Miriam and Aaron chastise Moses not only concerning his leadership but also because he married a woman of another ethnicity. God's punishment can be understood as both a reprimand of Miriam and Aaron for questioning Moses' leadership and for speaking against Moses' marriage. Some people interpret this passage as evidence that God supports interracial relationships. Third, God acknowledges that God is revealed to people other than Moses via dreams and visions; but it is only with Moses that God speaks so intimately. Moses' close association with God should make others wary of how they approach God. But neither Miriam nor Aaron seem to have that holy fear.

- How do you seek to be in God's presence? In what ways do you approach God?

Road Signs

- **Wilderness of Paran** (PAY-ruhn): This is an Israelite campsite after leaving Sinai. It is believed to have been located south of Canaan.
- **Hobab** (HOH-bab): He was the son of Jethro (also called Raguel or Reuel) the Midianite, Moses' father-in-law
- **Taberah:** This is the Hebrew word for "burning."
- **Homer:** This was an ancient Hebrew unit of capacity equivalent to about 10 bushels or 100 gallons of our modern-day measure.
- **Kibroth-hattaavah** (KIB-roth-huh-TAY-uh-vuh): This is Hebrew for "graves of lust."
- **Cushite:** This is someone from the land of Cush, which if it still existed, would be located in present-day Ethiopia.

Numbers

4 Prayer

Gracious God, we thank you that men and women of all races are made in your image and that you desire us to celebrate the beauty and gift of your diverse creation. Amen.

When we gather to worship God, we use more than our voices and more than the Bible. What were the various symbols of worship described in chapters 7 and 8 by which the Israelites also worshiped God? Then take a quiz at *amazingbiblerace.com.*

I Spy Something ... Scary
Numbers 13–16

1 Scouting the Terrain

Trailblazers

- **God**
- **Moses**
- **Caleb and Joshua**
  (Israelite spies who are among 12 dispatched to Canaan)

God commands Moses to send out twelve spies to check out Canaan, the land God has promised to give the Israelites. So Moses sends them out with instructions to bring back a report about the land, the people, the town, and just about everything else. The spies spend forty days away; and when they return, all but two of them have negative things to say. Everyone but Joshua and Caleb reports the dangers and threat of Canaan's inhabitants, suggesting that the Israelites will be unable to defeat them and conquer the Promised Land. At the sound of this news, the rest of the Israelites begin to cry for a leader to take them back to Egypt, instead of to Canaan where the inhabitants might kill them. Imagine the slap in the face to God, that after all this, they want to go back to slavery in Egypt. God becomes angry with the Israelites and wants to put them all to death; but Moses pleads on their behalf, seeking God's forgiveness by saying that God's reputation is at stake if God kills the Israelites. What will the neighbors think of such a God, who frees people, makes them promises, and then kills them before the promises come true? God listens to Moses' plea for forgiveness but still punishes the disobedient Israelites. When the Israelites hear how God is going to punish them, they try to repent to save their skins by going up toward Canaan. And they go even after Moses' warns them that it's too late and that going to Canaan now will result in their death.

- If God forgave the Israelites, does it make sense that God still punished them? Explain your answer.

- What are some things that the Israelites have seen or experienced up until this moment that should have left them virtually fearless? Why, do you think, were they afraid?

3 Switchback

It seems as though no one trusts anyone else in the community. Most of the Israelites do not seem to trust God; and after the spies return from Canaan, the people are more open to hearing the bad news than anything faithfully reassuring that Caleb and Joshua have to say. Aaron and Miriam have already complained against Moses; and as the book continues, even some of the Levites begin to complain about their position and about Moses and Aaron's leadership. No one is satisfied with God's provision and direction. Everyone seems to want more for themselves: security, power, leadership, and food. All of these unfortunate human tendencies are not particular to the ancient Israelites alone; in so many ways, people of God to act out in similar fashion today.

• It appears that following God doesn't make a person perfect. Do you think that God expects us to be perfect, or is God happy when we try our best to be perfect and learn from our mistakes along the way?

• What were the spies implying about God by their reports on Canaan?

• Why, do you think, was God was so angry at the Israelites this time?

With your team, write a skit that portrays a day in the life of the "perfect Christian." Start from the moment he or she wakes up to the moment he or she goes to bed. Include all of the things he or she might say and do in an ordinary day. When the skit is complete, perform it for your youth group or videotape it and upload it to *amazingbiblerace.com.* Your Race Director has to see it for you to get the points.

Remember that God is more concerned about the way we love God than about whether or not we are perfect.

4 Prayer

Dear God, sometimes it is hard to trust the things you promise us through your Son Jesus Christ— things such as your constant love for us, your forgiveness of our sins, and your ability to make us new creations through faith in Jesus. Help us live our lives as though we really do believe those promises. Amen.

Aaron the Priest
Numbers 17–20

1 Scouting the Terrain

There has been so much grumbling amongst the Israelites, about leadership and who is holy enough to lead the people, that God decides to put an end to it once and for all. God instructs Moses to collect a staff from every tribe and from Aaron, who is head of the Levites, and to place the staff before God in the tent of the covenant. If someone's staff blooms, he is the man God has chosen to be leader. Of course, Aaron's staff is the only one that blooms; and God makes Aaron's staff a reminder that death will come to all who would threaten his leadership. The people are terrified at this. Instead of rejoicing in the fact that God has appointed someone to intercede on their behalf, to serve as their permissible access to God, they complain as usual—this time with fears that God will kill them all. It's as though they miss the whole point.

Trailblazers
- **God**
- **Moses**
- **Aaron**

In response to the people's cries of fear, God instructs Aaron in his responsibilities as priest. Aaron and his sons are the only ones given the gift to preside over the sanctuary, all the sacrifices, and offerings. They are responsible for protecting the rest of the Israelites from the dangers of God's holiness. The other Levites will serve Aaron and his sons in the general duties related to the Tabernacle, but they are not allowed into the holy places or to touch the altar. God will ensure that the priests and other Levities are provided with all of their needs so that they don't have to worry about anything besides serving God through their duties. This provision comes by the required offerings and tithes that the Israelites make to the priests and Levites.

- How would you feel if God made you a priest like Aaron?

- Can you think of any reasons why God's holiness could be considered so dangerous? Explain.

2 NOW READ NUMBERS 17–20.

③ Switchback

There's a lot of talk about life and death in these books. God is holy, and holiness is life. Death is considered an offense to God's holiness. So a lot of the ritual cleansing is to ensure that the Israelites can remain in God's presence.

God also takes offense when Moses and Aaron fail to trust that God will indeed provide water for the Israelites. As a result of their lack of faith, God punishes Moses and Aaron by telling them they will not live to enter the Promised Land.

• Did you ever stop to consider the idea of God's being offended? How does it feel to be offended?

• What are some things in our society that you believe might be offending God?

④ Prayer

Dear God, help us see our responsibilities as Christians to love and serve one another as a gift made possible by your love for us. Amen.

Road Signs

• **Holy things:** These are certain sacrificial offerings.
• **Redemption price:** This is the price paid as a substitution for God's claim of firstborn humans and unclean animals.
• **Tithe:** This is the mandatory tax, equal to one tenth of their income, that the Israelites had to make to the Temple.
• **"A red heifer ... on which no yoke has been laid":** This is a young cow that has never carried anything.
• **The water for cleansing:** This is the special concoction, made from the ashes of the sacrificed heifer, that cleansed those defiled by contact with the dead.
• **Kadesh** (KAY-dish): This was a city south of Canaan.
• **Meribah** (MER-ih-bah): Moses named this place "testing" because it is where the Israelites tested God's faithfulness and provision.
• **Mount Hor:** This is the mountain top where Aaron dies and God transfers the duty of high priest to Aaron's son Eleazar.

Water Break

Wow, it's the end of another week! Look how far you've already come. This week's reading has been a little difficult, with all of the facts and figures; but we hope that in the midst of it, you have learned something new about God. Great work so far!

Hey, Look! A Talking Donkey
Numbers 21–24

1 Scouting the Terrain

The Israelites leave the wilderness behind and spend time on the plains of Moab, preparing to enter and conquer Canaan. This section is full of battles with foreign kings; talking donkeys; poisonous serpents that both kill and heal; and our fierce leader, Moses, hearing of his impending death. But before the Israelites leave the wilderness behind, they offer up one last complaining bout that rouses the anger of God and leads to their destruction. This time, the people complain because they are sick of what God has provided. Can you believe that? It's not even a complaint of necessity, just one of dissatisfaction. They want the food variety of Egypt. It is almost as if they look back on Egypt, the place where they were enslaved, as the "land of milk and honey." As you can imagine, God is angry and punishes them—this time by sending poisonous snakes to bite them. When the Israelites seek God's forgiveness, they beg Moses to pray for them. God hears Moses' prayer and provides healing via a bronze snake coiled around a pole. The people must look at the serpent to be healed.

Trailblazers

- **God**
- **Moses**
- **Balaam**
- **Balak**

- Do you think that it's strange that the serpent can be both an object of destruction and an object of healing? What seems to make the difference?

- It seems that the Israelites have selective memory. They remember the food of Egypt but not the harsh conditions. Can you think of an example when your own selective memory made you long for the wrong things?

Racing Tip

Does the image of the serpent coiled around a pole remind you of any modern-day symbols? Here's a hint, think about organizations that help people.

98

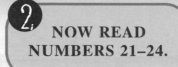

3. Switchback

There are several things to take from these chapters. The Israelites don't seem to be aware of what's going on between Balaam and Balak. 1) God protects the Israelites and remains faithful even when they are unaware of it; 2) God uses someone outside of the covenant; 3) God is faithful; 4) God provides for us in so many ways that we often do not even know about; 5) sometimes God provides from the most unlikely source, the person we least expect to be used by God.

• Can you think of a time when you experienced God's presence from an unlikely source?

• Is there anything in these chapters you have read that disturbs you? What images or portrayals surprise you?

Road Signs

• **Book of the Wars of the Lord:** This was the collection of war poems that depicted Israelite victories as God's doing.
• **Balak** (BAY-lak) **son of Zippor** (ZIP-or)**:** a Moabite king who was worried about the Israelites' population growth and military threat
• **Balaam** (BAY-luhm) **son of Beor** (BEE-or)**:** a prophet from Mesopotamia used by God to protect the Israelites.

Numbers

4. Prayer

Dear God, you are constantly giving and extending mercy, grace and protection. Please help us be grateful for the many ways you provide for us, both the ways we know about and the ways we do not. Amen.

Making Census of It All
Numbers 25–27

① Scouting the Terrain

Directly following a tale about how God uses a stranger to the covenant to protect Israel, we read the story of how strangers to the covenant threaten Israel's very existence. Some of the Israelites have become attached to the foreign god Baal. It seems that they have quickly forgotten the first commandment, "You shall have no other gods before me." The Numbers passage uses the word *yoked* to describe the relationship between the Israelites and the god Baal. This implies a deep intimacy. The text says that the Israelites joined in sacrifices to Baal, ate with the fellow Baal worshipers, and so became "yoked."

The second story of Israelite offense centers on God's jealousy for Israel. This time it involves an Israelite man who marries a Midianite woman. Both are killed by Phinehas the priest, and God is no longer angry with the rest of the Israelites.

Trailblazers

• **God**
• **Moses**
• **Phinehas**
• **Mahlah, Noah, Hoglah, Milcah, and Tirzah** (daughters of Zelophehad)

• How would an observer be able to tell if Christians are "yoked" to God?

• What do you think of the idea that God is a jealous God? Is it the same way we use the word jealousy? Of what do you think God is jealous?

Road Signs

• **Shittim** (SHIH-tim): This is the place where the Israelites stopped and mingled with Moabite women.

• **Baal of Peor:** In this context, it was a local god of the Moabites. But traditionally Baal is a Canaanite god.

• **Phinehas** (FIN-ee-huhs): He was a priest, the son of Eleazar, and the grandson of Aaron.

• **Covenant of Peace:** This was a promise to protect Phinehas from Midianites seeking revenge.

• **Covenant of perpetual priesthood:** This promised that all of Phinehas's descendants shall be honored with the role of priesthood.

③ Switchback

The last round of adult Israelites who left Egypt and complained all along the way have died off with the incident of Baal of Peor. Remember how God punished them earlier by telling them they would not live to enter the land? Moses and Eleazar take a new census of the people, thus pointing out the second generation of Israelites, the ones God promised would reach Canaan. Notice it is now Moses and Eleazar, no longer Aaron because he died at Mount Hor. Eleazar is the new high priest. The second census moves the story along and indicates that the people are well on the way to reaching Canaan once they cross the Transjordan. The story is also the backdrop for another important subplot, the inheritance of the daughters of Zelophehad. It is rare that women are given the center stage in Hebrew Scripture and even more rare that they are portrayed to be so assertive and intelligent. The last time we saw this was with Tamar back in Genesis 38. But here, the five women, Mahlah, Noah, Hoglah, Milcah, and Tirzah, defy traditional customs and request that they receive their father's inheritance, since there are no men left in their family. Usually, the men received all the property. Because of their boldness, God institutes a new law permitting women to hold property in certain circumstances.

- It is easy to assume that the genealogy of the Israelite tribes is not important. What do you think *could* be important about knowing who has made up our families, and what type of characters came before us?

- Where else is there a change of leadership besides that of Aaron to Eleazar?

② NOW READ NUMBERS 25–27.

hurdle If you're struggling through the census summary in Chapter 26, go to *amazingbiblerace.com* for some help. You can check out some interesting info and take a short quiz to help you get over that hurdle.

Numbers

④ Prayer

Gracious and merciful God, may we find the courage to approach you boldly with our requests and trust in your mercy and wisdom to grant us the things we truly need and can faithfully manage. Amen.

Israelites: The Next Generation
Numbers 28–30

1 Scouting the Terrain

As the second generation is ushered in, Moses has to teach them the ways of holy worship and sacrifice. These new leaders—priests and laypeople—must understand that God requires their lives to be marked by worship and obedience. The times for festivals, sacrifice, and worship cycle through the year. Even though these responsibilities fall mainly on the priests, all of the Israelites need to hear these words so that they can keep one another accountable.

The other piece of this section reveals more ways by which men and women were differentiated. It is helpful to understand the cultural and historical aspects of the societies written about in the Scripture. Men had the final say in a lot of the decisions women made. Fathers and husbands could even decide against the vows women made to God. Such subordination seems odd in a culture where we strive for gender equality and celebrate the accomplishments of women.

Trailblazers
- God
- Moses

- What worship-related customs and traditions have been passed down to you?

- Can you think of any examples of cultures and religions in which women still play a very subordinate role?

2 NOW READ NUMBERS 28–30.

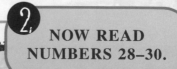

③ Switchback

Our time is not our own, but so often we live as though what we do with our time is entirely up to us. Even the way we talk about the concept of time shows how we imagine that it is something at our disposal. We say things like "don't waste my time," "let's kill some time," "She was talking so much to buy herself time," "Time is money," and "There's no time to spare." But life in God's kingdom suggests something entirely different about time. There is always more than enough time to live in the way that God calls us. There is time for fellowship with other people, time to worship God with praise, time to pray to God, and time to witness the many ways God comes to us in each day. Under God's reign, there is always an appointed time for celebration and for solemn recognition. There is always time to rest, to honor the Sabbath, and to be still and know that God is God.

- What are three things for which you wish to have time? Why are these things important to you?

- What would you have to change in your life to make time for these three things?

 Make a chart showing when the Israelites were instructed to mark time by worship and sacrifice. Begin your chart with the time periods of the day, then the week, the month, and the year. Then go to *amazingbiblerace.com* to take a quiz to check your work.

④ Prayer

Dear God, please help us make time for the things that would draw us closer to you. And help us recognize the appointed times in our lives to celebrate your faithfulness and to mourn over the darkness still in our world. Amen.

War With the Midianites
Numbers 31–33

1 Scouting the Terrain

God's instructs the Israelites to battle opposing peoples and tells them how to settle in the Promised Land. The land will need to be divided between the Israelite tribes. The Reubenites and the Gadites, part of Manasseh's tribe, are herders by trade; and they prefer the fertile land of the Transjordan. So Moses and Eleazar strike a deal with them. If these tribes agree to fight the necessary holy wars and help the other Israelite tribes reach Canaan, they may keep the fertile land they have asked for. The welfare of the entire community comes before individual needs and desires.

The first call to holy war is the attack against the Midianites as holy vengeance for how they led the Israelites astray at Baal Peor (remember the story from yesterday.) The writers use this story to tell us about the rules of holy war: what to do with the captured people, the material possessions, and the animals. You will learn more about this topic when you read Deuteronomy. The leader of the war, surprisingly, is not Joshua the warrior, but Moses, Eleazar, and Phinehas.

Trailblazers

- **God**
- **Moses**
- **Eleazar**
- **Phinehas**
  (Eleazar's son, also a priest)

Road Signs

- **"Gathered to your people":** This was a term that meant "to die."

WEEK
10
◇
DAY
4

• Does anything surprise you about the Israelite war plans?

• Other than calling up the Israelite army against them, how else could God have punished the sinful Midianites? Why, do you think, did God choose this action?

3 Switchback

Chapter 33 rehashes the entire Israelite journey from Egypt to their current campsite in Moab by the Transjordan. Notice the military tone of the chapter. The journey march is marked by places where the Israelites were disobedient and places where God continued to prove faithful. Now the Israelites are about to enter the Promised Land, and there will be additional rules of living to be learned. Life in Canaan will be different from life in the wilderness. Additional battles will be fought in Canaan. War is certainly a central focus of the Book of Numbers and seems a necessary part of the fulfillment of God's promises to the Israelites.

Christians have many different opinions about whether war is ever a right course of action. Some Christians believe that no form of violence is ever a faithful action. They believe that Jesus teaches nonviolence and that the act of killing is a sin against the God of love and peace. Other Christians believe in a "just war," that under certain pre-determined conditions, war is the most faithful course of action, necessary to promote God's peace and justice in the world for all people.

• How does religion play a role in the war against the Midianites? What roles do the religious men play in the war?

• How is this depiction of war different from how we usually think about wars in modern times?

• Where in the text do you see evidence of God's direct involvement in the wars?

4 Prayer

Gracious Lord, help us be people who seek peace and not war. We pray for people who live in neighborhoods and countries where there is violent fighting all around them. Protect them, and bring them peace. Amen.

• Do you believe that war is ever justified? Why?

Numbers

The Land Is Ours
Numbers 34–36

1 Scouting the Terrain

The final chapters of Numbers concern the logistics of claiming the land, organizing the tribes, making civil laws about homicide, and revising laws about tribal inheritance. But the main point of all this is that God has truly been faithful to God's word. The promise of land is being delivered to Israel. In Canaan, the Israelites will no longer be a nomadic people, they will be rooted; and so all the lessons given and learned during the wilderness journey will be modified as necessary for their new home. There will still be a sacred order to tribal living and settlement. The Levites will continue to play the role of protecting the Israelites. But instead of being placed in the inner circle of the camp by the Tabernacle, they will be given their own cities. And some of those cities will be places of refuge for criminal suspects and offenders.

As the Israelites prepare to enter the new land, it seems essential that they know how to deal with bloodshed that occurs in their midst. Remember that death is an offense to a holy God. Even when God demands death as punishment, all of the people or things associated with death must be ritually cleansed before they can reenter the presence of God and God's holy community.

• Do you remember the earliest story of the Bible in which we learned that murder was an offense to God and to the land?

2. NOW READ NUMBERS 34–36.

3 Switchback

Healthy land is a gift. It provides a place to build a home, to cultivate crops for food, to feed livestock, and to ensure some security for future generations. People are responsible for using God's gifts wisely and for constantly recognizing that the Gift-Giver is never far from the gift. However, it is easy to lose sight of just how important healthy land still is today. Most of us live in communities where we have no direct access to land as a means of providing food and financial security. When we imagine where our food comes from, most of us immediately think of the supermarket. But there are people, farmers in your state or a nearby state, who understand what a precious gift good land really is. And some people, in places such as Latin America, struggle to make a living because their families' land has been illegally taken away from them, sometimes by the shedding of innocent blood. God still calls us as Christians to recognize the gift of land and to find ways to care for the earth around us.

• How can you find out more about where your food really comes from?

• Do you know where coffee comes from or whether the coffee farmers are paid enough to live on? Think about these things. Caring about justice is all part of being a faithful Christian.

• This narrative depicts God's approval of capital punishment, a highly controversial topic among both Christians and non-Christians. What do you think about the use of capital punishment today?

4 Prayer

God, thank you for all of the gifts of nourishment you provide. Help us pay more attention to where our food comes from and the chain of people affected by how we consume goods. Amen.

Water Break

Now you have made it through Numbers! Well done! You too are well on your way to the Promised Land. But first, we need to read about how to live in that land. Deuteronomy gives us Moses' final speech to the people and the final book of the first fie books of the Bible. Even though we are not Israelites, we will learn a lot from the next book, about worshiping God.

Ready, Set, Go
Deuteronomy 1–3

1 Scouting the Terrain

Today's reading serves as an introduction to the Book of Deuteronomy. Moses reminds the people of how God called them to set out from Mount Horeb after they had received the Ten Commandments. He retells the story of how the first generation of Israelites came to die in the wilderness. The spies who were sent out to survey the land returned and instilled in the Israelites a lack of faith in God's ability to defeat the foreign nations. God's anger was kindled and God vowed that no adult over the age of twenty would live to enter the Promised Land. Moses even blames them for God's anger against him and the fact that he will not live to enter Canaan. Joshua will be the new leader of the people. Moses also narrates their war victories as God's provision.

Trailblazers
- **God**
- **Moses**
- **Joshua**

Road Signs
- **Mount Horeb:** This is another name for Mount Sinai.

• Why might it be important, right before they finally enter the Promised Land, for the Israelites to hear the story of their past, beginning with life at Mount Sinai/Horeb?

What qualities do you think make a good leader and why? What qualities did Moses possess? Reviewing all that you've read thus far, consider Moses as a leader. Make a list of important events in his life and how he performed as a leader of the Israelites. After your research, go to *amazingbiblerace.com* to take a quiz about Moses.

3 **Switchback**

Moses has been an interesting character
in the biblical narratives. His life was spared
as an infant; and he grew up in the Pharaoh's house, with all of the privilege
that wealth affords. But that didn't stop him from trying to be a man of
justice, even if he tried by the wrong means. Remember that Moses killed an
Egyptian man who was attacking a Hebrew slave. Even then, Moses had
courage. Who knew just how much he was going to need that courage for the
events God had planned for his life? The added element that God gave him
was the assurance that God would be with him. Moses needed faith and
courage to fulfill God's plans. When things didn't seem to be going well,
when the people complained, and when Moses himself was tired and fed up,
it was still his faith in God's words and God's action and his courage to be
obedient despite how things looked, that got them all through. This shows
that our successes in life are by the grace of God and that God still desires
for us to actively and faithfully work toward the goals God sets for us.

• What goals has God set for you?

4 **Prayer**

*Dear God, grant us
courage to seek
justice in our
communities. And as
injustice has many
faces, give us the
eyes to recognize
those places where
we can act to help
neighbor, a friend, a
classmate and
especially the
strangers among us.
Amen.*

Deuteronomy

Catch Your Breath

There's a popular saying in our culture: "Don't
cry over spilt milk." This a way of saying,
"Forget about the past." Sometimes it's true, we
should forget about the past and move on in our
lives. But there are also times when it is
important to remember the past to help us live
better lives in the future. Can you think of an
example from your own life, when remembering
things from your past was helpful?

Remember to Love the Lord Your God
Deuteronomy 4–7

① Scouting the Terrain

Today's reading includes a beautiful, heartfelt speech about the importance of keeping God's commands. The Israelites will be a witness to the nations, attesting to God's faithfulness, God's holy and just order of things, God's wisdom, and God's love. People will see and declare that the God of Israel is unlike any other god. It is also a beautiful speech about raising children in the faith, in the knowledge and love of God. Children are society's memory banks, to whom stories are told; and truths, values, and convictions live on for future generations.

Trailblazers
- **God**
- **Moses**

Moses reminds the Israelites not to make idols of anything. How could they make a god to worship when nothing they create could replace the living God of Abraham, Isaac, and Jacob? God creates everything. The bottom line is that people must worship only the Creator and never worship created things or beings. Moses tells the people to realize what an amazing and unheard-of thing their faith journey has been. There has never been word of any other god who has performed the works that their God has and who has claimed a nation so completely and faithfully without any merit of the people. The only reason Israel is victorious in anything is because of God. Remembering this fact will affect their attitudes toward other nations, toward God's commands, and toward one another.

- Do you have any family stories, values, or convictions that have been passed on to you?

- Does the fact that everything you have is a gift from God affect the way you relate to other people and to God? How so?

② NOW READ DEUTERONOMY 4–7.

③ Switchback

There are many significant aspects to these few chapters. So much is packed in that it's important to highlight a few key things. Simply, if Israel is faithful to God, the Israelites will reap the promised rewards: long life in the land, prosperity, and many descendants. But if they are unfaithful, they will die, will be scattered to other nations, will be enslaved again, and will be forced to worship dead gods. Deuteronomy 6:4-9 is known as the *Shema,* which is Hebrew for "hear" or "listen." Notice the active verbs used to describe the *Shema: Hear,* Israel; *love* the Lord; *keep* these words, *recite* them; *talk* about them; *bind* them on your hand; *fix* them to your forehead; and *write* them. These verbs suggest that our bodies, our homes, and our conversations should reflect our love and commitment to God. Did you know that Jewish people still adhere to the *Shema* today? Some Jewish households even have a mezuzah on their front door frames or somewhere near the entrance to their homes.

• How does every aspect of your life reflect your commitment to God?

Road Signs

• **Mezuzah** (muh-ZOO-zuh): This is a small piece of parchment on which the Scripture passages Deuteronomy 6:4-9 and 11:13-21 and the word *Shaddai* (God) are written. This parchment is rolled up and put in a small container that is nailed to the front door frames of Jewish households as a sign of their faith and their conformance with Jewish Law.
• **Shema** (SHEE-muh): This is the Hebrew word for "hear" or "listen."

④ Prayer

Gracious Lord, you still desire us to love you with all our hearts, minds, and souls. Help us remember that loving you is an action, not just a feeling; and teach us to love boldly with our words, with our bodies, and within our relationships. Amen.

Rewards and Consequences
Deuteronomy 8–11

1 Scouting the Terrain

Trailblazers
- God
- Moses

These are chapters about rewards and consequences, about forgetfulness and prideful temptation, and about God's training ground for forming followers. Moses reminds the Israelites of their stubborn nature and the sins they have committed against God in the wilderness. Little did they know that the wilderness was a time of God's testing and training. God wanted to form the Israelites into humble and trusting children who recognize their ultimate dependence on God for survival and flourishing. But just like human beings today, the Israelites repeatedly failed the tests. These narratives serve to remind us of human faithlessness and God's unfaltering faithfulness. We didn't even think about how the Israelites met the need for clothes and shoes. And clearly, as Moses reminds them, neither did they. But God provides in so many ways and often takes care of our needs before we even realize that we have a need.

We are made in God's image, and therefore we can accomplish lots of things. But there is always a temptation to forget God's good works, especially when things are going well in our lives. If we, as well as the Israelites, were better about remembering God's faithfulness, we would realize that the responsibility of witness and praise of God's works rests on those who have known God firsthand and have directly benefited from God's love and mercy. And part of being a faithful witness to God's work is following God's example of caring for strangers and those in need.

- Can you think of a time in your family's life when God met your needs? Explain.

- Can you think of a difficult time that you went through but somehow it was used to form you into a new and better person? Explain.

2 NOW READ DEUTERONOMY 8–11.

3 Switchback

Memory is an interesting thing. All through the wilderness journey, the Israelites remember Egypt as a place worthy of returning. They recall the food, the apparent security, and the sense of knowing what lay ahead of them. However, they fail to remember the slaughter of the Hebrew children; the cruelty of Pharaoh and the taskmasters; and even the faithfulness of God, who led them out of captivity and provided for them during their long journey. Now, on the verge of entering the Promised Land, Moses has to remind them to use their memory faithfully. They will be tempted to forget the lessons of the wilderness and how God had provided for them. They will most likely readily remember their hunger and thirst, their fear of battle, God's punishment of disobedient Israelites, their fatigue and impatience. God knows all of this about human memory; and that is why, from the very beginning, God institutes times of the year when Israel is to remember God's actions through their fasts, festivals, and offerings.

Road Signs

- **Anakim** (AN-uh-kim): These were Canaanite people believed to be giants.
- **"Circumcise the foreskin of your heart"**: This is a way of telling the Israelites to open their minds and seek to do God's will.

- Worship is an act of remembering rightly. How do the details of your Sunday worship at church help you remember rightly?

- Can you point to specific aspects of your worship service that help foster your community's memory of what it means to be a follower of Christ?

4 Prayer

Dear God, you know that our memories can serve to hurt or to heal. Please help us remember the birth, life, death, and resurrection of Jesus Christ and how we have been baptized into such a life. Amen.

God Is a Jealous God
Deuteronomy 12–14

1 Scouting the Terrain

One of the key things the Israelites must do is destroy any trace of foreign gods, including their places of worship. Only then will God show them the place where God desires to be worshiped. The Israelites should not even raise the question about the foreign gods; because as the old saying goes, "Curiosity killed the cat." Asking questions can easily lead to trying to imitate the false worship practices. God has shown them how God is to be worshiped. There is nothing else for them to know or to do that God has not already instructed them on. Moses keeps using some variation of the phrase "whom you have not known" when referring to the Israelites being tempted to follow other gods. Something is truly significant about God's relationship with God's people. Unlike false gods, the God of Abraham, Isaac, and Jacob seeks out a relationship with those whom God loves. God desires intimate relationships and reveals God's self in order to love and be loved by God's children. Turning away from God or enticing others to do so results only in death. The community takes active part in killing the person who has gone astray or who has led others astray. Notice again how the Israelites are formed as a community of people and not just individuals looking out for themselves.

Trailblazers
• **God**
• **Moses**

• Why, do you think, is it important that, as Christians, we study the Hebrew Scriptures and learn about the Israelites' journey with God?

2 NOW READ DEUTERONOMY 12–14.

③ Switchback

These three chapters pretty much focus on Moses' teaching the Israelites to avoid the temptation of apostasy (denying God) and following false gods. Every aspect of daily life is determined by God's desire and will for the Israelites. Even the details of what, how, when, and where they eat have significance for worship and obedience. But the provision allowed for those who live far away from the appointed place of worship and sacrifice points to another level of meaning. The details and commands behind the daily Israelite life stem from the love of God. Ultimately, God desires to remain in intimate relationship with God's people. That's why the Israelites have to ensure that they are obedient and will listen to all God instructs. The instructed ways are the only ways that make it possible for sinful humans to be in relationship with a divine and holy God.

• What makes it possible for us to have a relationship with God?

• Think about your daily routine and lifestyle in general. What are some ways in which you work on "knowing" God? Is there anything that gets in your way of having a close relationship with God?

Road Signs

• **Omens or portents:** These are foresights or indications of future happenings, either good or bad.

④ Prayer

Dear God, remind us that our ideas of "knowing you" are reflected in how we live our lives each day. Amen.

Deuteronomy

Benevolence, Fairness, Justice
Deuteronomy 15–18

1 Scouting the Terrain

"Open your hand to the poor and needy neighbor in your land." This quotation from Chapter 15 is the crux of the next four chapters. The previous chapter ended with an important word on God's care for the needy. This section calls people to care for one another, providing the needs of the poor, the orphans, widows, and strangers who live in the land. We, as readers, learn that God is well aware of the pain and suffering of people in this world. God recognizes that the world is no longer as God intended it to be upon its creation. People will always hunger, thirst, and need in a variety of other ways. As followers of God, it is our responsibility to seek to always care for those in need in the ways we can. Just like the Israelites, we too are called to be pursuers of justice. They are not to forget where their many blessings come from and how they (and we) did nothing to deserve God's favor. A blessing is a gift; and likewise, they are to return God's gift by extending both deserved and undeserved blessings upon others.

Trailblazers
- **God**
- **Moses**

• When was the last time you received an undeserved gift?

• When was the last time you gave someone an undeserved gift?

• Did you feel any difference between being the gift-receiver and the gift-giver? Explain your answer.

2 NOW READ DEUTERONOMY 15–18.

3 Switchback

Being a leader is not easy. We've already seen what a tough time Moses had with the people and, sometimes, even with what God wanted him to do. And it's not always easy to follow a leader and trust his or her judgment, especially when you think that you could do a better job! The Israelites have to respect and honor the people whom God appoints as leaders. The judges, priests, and kings are supposed to represent God's ways and provide honest and just rulings and decisions. The Israelite king will stand out from all other kings, because God will guide him. He will be required to read God's laws on a daily basis to remind himself of whom he serves and for why he is king. This practice will also help keep him humble.

• How do you define the word *justice*? How, do you think, is your definition different from God's definition? How is it similar?

• Is there a leader or a person in a position of authority whom you have a hard time giving the proper respect? What is it that makes it difficult to respect this person?

4 Prayer

Dear God, very often your sense of justice looks a lot like grace. Sometimes we don't get the punishments we deserve for our behavior. You lavish us with blessings even when we ignore those in need right in our own communities. You sent your Son to die for the sins we've committed. Please teach us more about your idea of justice. Amen.

Water Break

Can you believe that you have been studying the Bible for eleven weeks already? That time has gone by quickly, hasn't it? You are halfway through Deuteronomy and almost done with the Pentateuch and almost done with the first leg of this race. By now, your training is paying off; and picking up your Bible and this book every day is easier and may be becoming a habit. Keep up the pace! Keep up the good work! And continue to walk closer to God!

The Legal System
Deuteronomy 19–22

1 Scouting the Terrain

These chapters of Deuteronomy focus on Moses' final words to the Israelites before they enter the Promised Land. Words about in legal and socio-economic justice, familial relationships, and rules for holy war. Establishing a legal/judicial system for the Israelites was unique for ancient times. The victim's family avenged most criminal acts, and there were few ways of determining guilt or innocence. So part of God's instructions to the Israelites includes securing safe places for criminals until they can be fairly tried by the elders of the community. The other reason for these places of refuge is to keep the land free of "blood guilt." Remember that the health of the land is related to the faithfulness of the people.

Trailblazers

• **God**
• **Moses**

The notion of holy war is to remind the Israelites that God's might and mercies are at the center of all their victories and that the Promised Land is a divine gift. The rules of battle include a blessing, a reminder by the priest that God wins battles, and an offering of peace to the enemy. Before going to battle, the soldiers are weeded out according to those who have mind-consuming responsibilities at home and based on their level of courage. Men who are afraid cannot go to war, because they could easily affect the courage of others. Fear is contagious.

• What do you think about the idea of holy war? Are there still wars fought in the name of God?

• What do you think of Christians who support pacifism (a commitment to non-violence)?

2 NOW READ DEUTERONOMY 19–22.

③ Switchback

At the heart of some laws is the respect for family unity and the recognition that the Israelite community was largely sustained by the familial economic system. Parents and firstborns must be given the respect and privilege due them. Even a female war captive was to be given time for mourning and lamenting the death of her parents.

However the flip-side of learning about Israelite family life is that we learn about the biblical-time cultural norms for how to treat women, which can sometimes be difficult to understand and accept. Women were not really given a say whether or not they wanted to marry a certain man. The suitor and the male head of the woman's household made marital decisions. Fortunately, there were some laws that ensured that women would be provided for financially even when other members of the family or society tried to ignore the few women's rights that did exist.

• What part of these Scriptures suggests that Israelite women had a respectable status and could not easily be unworthy?

④ Prayer

Gracious God, forgive us the many things we do in your name that may not actually have anything to do with your will, especially when we act violently toward others both physically and emotionally. And where we are blind to your will, give us new vision. Amen.

While many of the Mosaic laws that you have read about seem be very different from our justice system and societal standards, some are similar. What similarities do you see? What are some of the laws you have read about that are either still in effect or seem to have influenced today's laws and rules of society? Go to *amazingbiblerace.com* to take a quiz.

Inclusion and Exclusion
Deuteronomy 23–26

1 Scouting the Terrain

A large portion of Deuteronomy is concerned with who is in and who is out. What makes someone part of the favored Israelite community, and where does hospitality and faithful remembrance play into things? This next section begins with a list of who can and can't be a part of the community. At the root of these boundaries are issues of sexual and physical standards of health and long-standing ethnic and political conflicts. Readers might be surprised to find the Egyptians on the invite list. Yet God says that Egyptian children of the third generation are permitted to the assembly of the Lord, because the Israelites were once aliens in Egypt and also because the Israelites would need the Egyptians as economic partners. However, people are also allowed into the community for compassionate and hospitable reasons—slaves are allowed to take refuge in Israelite cities.

Trailblazers
• **God**
• **Moses**

Although other boundaries are established that reflect continuous issues of justice, compassion, and respect, these chapters can seem confusing because there does not appear to be any unifying thread holding it all together. But the details all speak to the wider goal of creating a community where people are treated fairly, where neighbors are respected and the importance of family acknowledged, where hospitality is a way of life, where the poor are remembered, and where non-human creation is cared for. And all of these things speak to what it means to worship the God of Abraham, Isaac, and Jacob.

• What kind of rules, spoken or unspoken, guide the faith communities of which you are a part?

• Are there specific ways in which the poor are remembered in your faith community? What are they?

2 NOW READ DEUTERONOMY 23–26.

③ Switchback

Chapter 26 is important because it rehashes the role of worship in the Israelite community and uses liturgy to draw connections between how God has acted, how God is acting, and how God will act. The chapter is an excellent example of how liturgy shapes our lives and forms us into certain kinds of people. The word *liturgy* literally means "the work of the people." In this sense, we understand it as the way people worship (show reverence) and as the way people work for the benefit of the community, recognizing God as the center of our lives. One significant role of liturgy is to remind worshipers of the communal story of which they are a part and of how each individual is responsible for continuing the story—in this case, the story of a covenant with the God of Israel.

- Based on the definition provided for *liturgy,* can you describe the liturgy of your church? Explain.

- Whose stories help you make sense of your own story? Do you even think of yourself as having a story?

Road Signs

- **"Those born of an illicit union":** Some scholars suggest that this refers to children born from incestuous relationships, or from persons whose familial relationship is so close that their union is illegal or forbidden by custom.
- **Mill, upper millstone:** This device consists of two abrasive stones, between which grain is ground into flour for making bread.
- **Weights and measures:** This is the means by which people set prices to sell their items.

Racing Tip

The duty of a deceased husband's brother was to continue the family name by bearing a child with the widow. (See also the story of Onan in Genesis 38:2-8.)

④ Prayer

Dear God, sometimes I forget that I do not write my own story and that I am already a part of a bigger story that you write. Please help me find my voice so that I can continue to tell the story of your love in my life. Amen.

Blessings and Curses
Deuteronomy 27–28

1 Scouting the Terrain

Trailblazers
- **God**
- **Moses**

Here begins the final charge of Moses to the people, a collection of warnings, blessings, and potential reasons for curses. It's a speech worthy of careful reading. The significance of this speech is highlighted by the fact that both Moses and the elders gather to deliver it and the fact it was delivered right before the Israelites crossed the Jordan to the Promised Land. It's almost as if the leaders were saying, "OK, we've told you all you need to do in order to be faithful followers of God; and so far, you all haven't been the greatest at it. But this is the real deal. You either choose to listen and adhere to the rules and end up happy and successful with God totally on your side, or you choose to play by your own rules and end up wishing that you were never born. Think about it and make up your mind because we're going in."

• Curses were declared publicly; however, most of the actions that led to curses were done without anyone else in the community knowing about them. So what was the point of publicly affirming punishments for offenses done secretly?

• How do you feel about the explanation that God's justice is the reason that good and bad things happen to people?

2 NOW READ DEUTERONOMY 27–28.

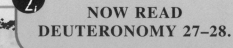

3 Switchback

The curses described appear exceedingly harsh and outnumber the blessings. However, it's important to remember that many scholars believe that this part of Deuteronomy was composed in various sections after the horrific events of the sixth century, when Jerusalem was captured. Many Israelites were forced to flee, were captured by enemies, and even sold themselves and their children into slavery. The horrors described are events actually believed to have befallen the Israelites. Believeing that God is just might have been a way to explain why such horrible things happened to them. It must be that God was justly repaying them for their disobedience.

Retelling about and interpreting these events also served to teach present-day Israelites what had happened in history due to the Israelites' disobedience. It also served to show that such horrors are not because Israel's God isn't powerful enough to defeat other gods and human enemies, rather they occurred because God is just.

- The theological attempt to explain why God permits evil is called theodicy. How do you make sense of evil in our world?

- What do you think of the Israelite explanation for the atrocities that happened to them?

4 Prayer

Dear God, I know that you are just and that you are love. But sometimes I can't understand why you let evil things happen in the world, especially when innocent people are involved. Help me trust even when I do not understand. Amen.

Racing Tip

Covering the stones with plaster (Deuteronomy 27:2) made for a better writing surface.

Recounting Our History
Deuteronomy 29–31

1 Scouting the Terrain

Israel's identity is intimately tied to the possession of land and to its relationship with God and its response to God's covenant. These chapters are again looking back to Israelite history, both with God and with humans. This portion of Deuteronomy was written to a people in exile. Now they had been defeated by enemy nations—most notably the Babylonians—and were exiled without land or hope, losing a sense of collective identity and wondering what was to become of them.

Trailblazers
- **God**
- **Moses**

The author uses past events to stir their memory of God's power and might. God had made a covenant with them at Mount Horeb and had led them through the wilderness into abundant blessing, and this God of Israel could do it again. This is a speech of hope, given to boost the morale and spirit of a defeated people in captivity. But at the center of such renewed faith and hope is the need for repentance and recommitment to God. The Israelites had to remember the ways in which their unfaithfulness had led to their loss of land, status, and divine favor. And as always, the actions of one generation of Israelites have repercussions for future generations. So the author is again laying before them the choice to choose life and blessing over death and curse.

- One way the Israelites denied God's sovereignty was by doubting that God could deliver them and that God had power over other lesser gods. Can you think of one way we deny God's sovereignty today? What is it?

2 NOW READ DEUTERONOMY 29–31.

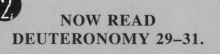

③ Switchback

These chapters make us think about how it is that we are ministered to during our own times of feeling hopeless, disappointed in ourselves, uncertain about God's purposes for us, or filled with thoughts of bleak possibilities for our future. So often, when we are down, we want to be left alone to wallow in our despair and sometimes to feel sorry for ourselves. Who wants to go to church or hear a sermon when our world has fallen apart? But that's when we most need those words of encouragement and hope. The author of these passages knew that.

And such thoughts are also affirmed by Paul, in the New Testament, in 1 Corinthians 1:25: "For God's foolishness is wiser than human wisdom, and God's weakness is stronger than human strength," and also in 2 Corinthians 12:9: "My grace is sufficient for you, for [God's] power is made perfect in [human] weakness."

- In what ways has turning to God helped you during times of despair in the past?

- What Scripture verses or songs do you find comforting?

Who in your community could use some encouragement or a reminder of hope and faith? Choose an act (or some acts) of kindness to encourage people in your community. Work with your team to lift someone's spirit. Be sure to take a photo or video of your outing, and upload it to *amazingbiblerace.com*.

④ Prayer

Dear God, you don't seem to judge our less-than-faithful thoughts and actions as we deserve. All too often, you shower us with grace. Help us choose the things that bring life, not out of fear of your judgment but out of love for you. Amen.

Moses' Farewell
Deuteronomy 32–34

1 Scouting the Terrain

It's hard to believe that these are the last three chapters of the Pentateuch. What a journey it has been, from Creation to calling to liberation to wilderness challenge to formation and law-giving to blessing and curse and now to the end of Moses' time as unmatchable leader.

Trailblazers
- God
- Moses
- Joshua

The final words of Moses are a mixture of poetry and song. Remember how Moses sang at the onset of Israelite freedom, right after they had crossed the Red Sea and God had defeated the Egyptians? How appropriate that Moses now ends with another song, on the verge of God's promise being fulfilled. The song of Chapter 33 has familiar themes of the consequences of obedience and disobedience. But it ends with a note of hope. A jealous God is a forgiving God. God's jealous actions are not simply for the sake of vengeance but also to jog the Israelites' memory, to remind them who is their real God, their Provider and Sustainer. And God is still concerned with being the one true and victorious God.

The last words of Moses serve as a benediction, a farewell blessing to the tribes, calling good will and God's will upon each of the twelve tribes. Moses is turning over his leadership to Joshua and giving the Israelites a final word of hope, encouragement, and assurance that God is still with them and will bless them and forgive them.

- Despite Moses' hard work as a leader enduring all he did with the stubborn Israelites, God still holds to God's word and denies Moses entrance into the Promised Land. How do you imagine Moses felt? What does this suggest about how we should understand God?

- What would be your final words to the Israelites on the verge of entering the Promised Land?

2 NOW READ DEUTERONOMY 32–34.